D1067892

WANG AN-SHIH

Practical Reformer?

PROBLEMS IN ASIAN CIVILIZATIONS

WANG AN-SHIH—PRACTICAL REFORMER? *Edited by John Meskill*

THE CHINESE CIVIL SERVICE—CAREER OPEN TO TALENT? *Edited by Johanna M. Menzel*

DEMOCRACY IN MODERN JAPAN—GROUNDWORK OR FACADE? *Edited by George O. Totten*

JAPAN 1931–1945—MILITARISM, FASCISM, JAPANISM? *Edited by Ivan Morris*

1857 IN INDIA—MUTINY OR WAR OF INDEPENDENCE? *Edited by Ainslee T. Embree*

Other volumes in preparation

PROBLEMS IN ASIAN CIVILIZATIONS

WANG AN-SHIH
Practical Reformer?

EDITED WITH AN INTRODUCTION BY

John Meskill

BARNARD COLLEGE

D. C. HEATH AND COMPANY • BOSTON

Table of Contents

Introduction

WHATEVER else might seem perennially exotic about Chinese civilization, there has never been anything strange about the wish of Chinese governments to maintain their power and preserve order in the country. Maintaining political power sometimes, as in the middle period of Chinese history with which these readings are concerned, depended upon an ability to withstand foreign enemies. On the face of the matter, that should not have been too difficult to do. China was by far the largest, richest, and most populous country of East Asia and simply in terms of resources ought to have been able to dominate any and all of her comparatively poor neighbors. In fact, however, a more effective threat to Chinese governments came from within the country, sometimes so weakening it that small foreign forces made Chinese greatness seem a myth. The internal weaknesses, about which much remains to be learned, seem to have recurred in several major dynasties and to have included economic, fiscal, and administrative difficulties. Economically, for example, there seem to have been movements toward the concentration of land in the hands of people or institutions able to avoid in different ways and degrees the payment of heavy taxes. Independent farmers declined in number, and the dispossessed might become marauding vagabonds, or excessively-pressed tenants who expressed their discontentment through uprisings. Fiscally, there was a tendency toward higher government expenditure, partly to maintain internal security, and lower revenues. Administratively there were a number of questions, one of which was the quality of officialdom, whose patterns of behavior too often worked against the health of the state. As dynasties grew older, movements along such lines might so disrupt national order that the government, especially affected and by then too weak to withstand the attacks of native or foreign foes, came down, most often not with a bang but a whimper.

For the many serious officials who saw these morbid processes at work and sought ways to stop them, the bureaucracy itself seemed a crucial weakness. There were reasons to believe that a stronger bureaucracy could do much to arrest or even cure the ailments. Not only was the bureaucracy the supreme political organization under the emperor, but also it carried the highest social prestige and represented considerable economic influence, since its members often came from landholding families. It could be expected to exert great influence, when it was determined to do so, through its political, social, and economic eminence; but even more important, the bureaucracy could represent and inculcate a morality which would go far toward solving difficulties that were essentially the result of men's inhumanity. The bureaucracy was the most educated group in Chinese society, and the education it received included one of the most persistent and noble themes of Chinese political thought, the theory that the power of a government depended on the acquiescence of the people. The maintenance of political power, therefore, came to be seen very much as the question of the achievement of a bureaucracy of competence, integrity, and moral awareness, which would lead to a regeneration of general economic, fiscal, and social strength. Whether the regeneration would come about naturally or would be devised by an invigorated government was a matter of dispute, but the central question almost always concerned government. One critical aspect of the problem was the finding of the right men for government (a subject taken up in Johanna M. Menzel's *The Chinese Civil Service: Career Open to Talent?*, a volume in this series).

Another aspect was the general question of the reform of society by government. How much could a highly-placed group of reformers alter conditions in a society of tens of millions of people? Some of the institutional difficulties facing reformers have been described by James T. C. Liu, in "An Early Sung Reformer: Fan Chung-yen" (in John K. Fairbank, ed. *Chinese Thought and Institutions*. University of Chicago Press, 1957, pp. 105–131). As he points out, the bureaucracy was the only effective forum of political discussion, and its highest executive officials could exert great influence on the emperor. Nevertheless, legitimate political power was the emperor's alone; the authority great ministers enjoyed was derived power, subject to the emperor's will. The major methods officials had of affecting political decisions were persuasion of the emperor and representing to him "public opinion," which for the most part may have been opinions voiced in the bureaucracy. Both these methods were employed in council with the emperor.

Any minister with a plan for government required the emperor's approval and probably substantial favorable "public opinion," both to influence the emperor and as assurance that important groups of the bureaucracy would cooperate in the plan,

If the plan called for far-reaching reforms in institutions and methods, special obstacles had to be overcome. The very scale of the changes proposed made it likely that other officials or the emperor would disagree on one point or another. The invention of new schemes and systems could be construed as an excessive dependence on the machinery of government or "laws," which smacked of Legalism, a harsh theory of impersonal government discredited for centuries. It could be argued that moral suasion, a strong element in Confucian thought, rather than systems was the proper business of an adviser of the emperor and the true way to a better society. The support of some officials would be lost over such issues. Others, perhaps many, governed by what might be called today a bureaucratic temperament, would remain uncommitted to new political goals, concerning themselves mainly with their orderly advancement in the organization. Still others would oppose the reforms for fear of economic and social loss.

Rallying important groups of the bureaucracy to the side of reform was a formidable task, but winning and keeping the emperor's confidence was no easier. Reformers were vulnerable to the charge that what they proposed defied tradition. It was no clinching argument to say, as modern bureaucratic reformers might, that the proposed changes would increase efficiency. It had also to be shown that they were in accord with the way of government of the classical past, and to an increasing degree in accord with the spirit of the founders of the dynasty. To go against this way meant not only to deny the most cherished values of Chinese civilization but to indicate unworthy motives, most likely an ambition for power for selfish ends. Habits of thought that stressed harmony more than a clash of opinions did not easily adjust to the existence of "factions" of men pushing their ideas at the expense of concord. The charge could be made outright, if the emperor did not sense it lying within much else that was said, that those who wished great change were greatly dissatisfied with the rule of the emperor himself.

There was a propensity in disputes at the Court to attack persons as much as positions. This was often clear in, for example, arguments over rites, which sometimes provided issues over which factional disputes on much broader grounds came to a head. After bitter arguments over, perhaps, what appellation was proper for the father of an emperor who was not the son of the previous emperor, the losers would be reviled and harassed not merely as wrong but as immoral. Questions of rites, often closely connected with the imperial family, may well have seemed crucial because they tested the depth to which the disputants were educated in tradition and because their resolution would be of intimate concern to the emperor. In other questions as well, however, the character of the men involved carried at least as much weight as the substance of the issue. The idea that government was by men more than by systems was well established, and men who proposed changes in systems were perhaps by that very fact open to criticism of themselves as keys to the meaning of their reforms.

There were many efforts to reform Chinese society in traditional times. The one that is the subject of this book certainly cannot stand for all of them, but it has the merit of being an especially comprehensive effort, in which problems of reform and reformers in the middle period of Chinese history are well set forth. It is also distinguished by its participants, for it happened that the age put forth an unusually large number of great men, whose concern in the effort gave it a feeling of great moment.

If there had been tourism in the eleventh century, almost any traveller to China must have been struck with a sense of prosperity and peace. The one country of China stretched a thousand miles north to south and east to west, a land of mountains, rich plains and great rivers. There was the stamp of humanity everywhere: busy commercial cities, a splendid capital, and canals, walls and roads of great age. The country as a whole seemed to be at work. Little that was apparent suggested that the nation was in a critical state.

Yet many of the most prominent statesmen of the Northern Sung dynasty (960–1126) felt that it was. What they saw, within the apparent productivity and stability, were chronic national difficulties. On the northern and northwestern borders strong "barbarian" nations, such as the Khitan tribes of Liao (907–1125) and the Tangut of Hsi Hsia (1038–1227), far from paying the Chinese emperor the proper allegiance, threatened to become invaders at any time. Large Chinese armies, maintained against this threat and for internal security, burdened finances. Finances were in difficulty anyway, for despite signs that the productivity of the country was great, it seemed impossible to collect sufficient revenues to meet expenditures. There were reports that the richness of the country brought little benefit to the peasantry, which indebtedness and taxes were oppressing. For the statesmen who took such conditions to be critical (many of the most prominent men and their followers in the bureaucracy did, but there is little evidence that officialdom as a whole felt a sense of urgency), there was a vital need for reforms. Once agreed on that, the would-be reformers had to face some difficult questions. What kinds of reforms would do the most good? What reforms were possible, and how could they be carried out? Who was to do the reforming? What ends should reform serve? The closer answers to such questions came to proposals for specific action, the more serious the possible consequences of the actions loomed, and the sharper differences of opinion grew. With the regime of Wang An-shih (1021–1086), opinions hardened into commitments, disagreements became hatreds, and a controversy arose which to this day stirs strong feelings in the hearts of many Chinese.

Wang An-shih was well known even before his arrival at the Court. He had written impressively on scholarly subjects from about the time of his passing the highest civil service examinations, and he had established a reputation for vigorous and successful administration in outlying posts. Moreover, he had submitted his famous Ten Thousand Word Memorial, parts of which comprise the first selection in this book, while still a young man of thirty-seven. When at last he came to the Court, he had already caught the attention of the young Emperor, Shen-tsung (r. 1068–1085), who had read his writings and was to give him indispensable support and authority.

Wang's view of the central issues confronting the Chinese government appeared in the Ten Thousand Word Memorial. For the most part, his argument followed lines that others had taken before him, though perhaps less forcefully. He saw the state ineffectual against its foreign enemies, disturbed by unrest within, depleting its resources, and prone to moral laxity. He regarded such conditions as of the greatest danger, a threat to the life of the dynasty itself. The most urgent need, he insisted, was to find, test, use, and retain competent officials, who could correct the weaknesses he had described. To do so, government must return to the principles of the ancient kings, examine them for their intent, and put them into practice, not necessarily through the same means as of old, but in ways suited to modern conditions and yet consonant with the intentions of old.

The Memorial also suggested an approach to government which, when Wang's program was underway, would contribute to a style of action his opponents found offensive and dangerous. Wang was interested in plans of action, for example, and he urged the Emperor to be prepared to support vigorously policies of which he approved. Of course, emperors were always responsible for acting, but in political thought generally and in previous Sung administrations specifically, considerable weight had been put on consultation and conference among advisers. In warning against inaction in the face of opposition, Wang was apparently calling upon the Emperor to associate himself much more positively with definite policies than his immediate predecessors had. A possible objection to this, as we have seen, was that the Emperor's support of a broad program and of the men who suggested it might appear to be giving government over to a single group or "faction" of officials. Wang's repeated references to opponents of certain plans as "opportunists" or "compromising" men suggested an intransigeance that might aggravate such a condition.

Wang's argument that men should be placed in positions for which they had special qualifications, being a defense of specialization, seems commonplace today, but it should be remembered that it ran against the dominant Chinese attitude of the time, which assumed that a man of high humanistic education had the capacity to fill a great variety of administrative positions. It may be only hindsight to see significance in this view of Wang's, but the matching of men to positions may have bespoken an interest in government as a machine, comprising both institutional and human parts. In this it seems to resemble a modern bureaucratic outlook.

The second, short selection, "Current Extravagance," reinforces some of the points of the Memorial, such as Wang's insistence on thrift and his conviction that the wealth of some men was acquired against the interests of the people and the government. More clearly than in the Memorial, however, he spoke of forceful state intervention and even punishment as remedies. Force and punishment were familiar enough in Chinese government, but that Wang made it his concern to steel the Emperor to the use of such means gave his message an unusual tone for a public pronouncement. One of the articles of Confucian political theory stressed the importance of example and education in leadership. Conversely, compulsion tended to be associated with the Legalist theories of a millenium before, theories which writers had held up as bad government ever after. The practice of compulsion might be one thing. Advocating it as an important method of government was another.

It is not known whether anyone, after reading Wang's memorial on the need for competent men, asked what the men must do, once they had been found. Wang soon demonstrated, however, that his plans called for a broad program of institutional reforms. So diverse were the "New Laws," as they have been called, and so technical some of them, that they have seldom been discussed comprehensively in English, nor will they be here. In general they aimed at changing fiscal, economic, and bureaucratic practices. Those that are at issue in selections in this book are usually adequately described when they come up. It should be noted that some of the writers represented in the following pages disagree on the workings and even the emphases of some of the reforms. For a number of reasons, there is not yet agreement on all the essential facts, as one would expect of an event of comparable importance in European history, and what happened is sometimes as much in dispute as what it signified. To indicate their nature, an outline of a few of the measures follows:

1. *Finance Planning Commission.* It was indicative of a major emphasis of the New Laws that one of the first of Wang's acts had to do with state finances. He established the new Commission, setting it above a Finance Commission (*san-ssu*) already existing, to study and recommend changes in fiscal matters. The new Commission formally proposed and administered many of the other measures inspired by Wang.

2. *Tax Transport and Distribution System.* Regional fiscal officials were empowered to use funds in government granaries (which until then had stored grain to be used to stabilize prices), to purchase goods for the government in the cheapest market with economy of transportation in mind; or to sell goods under comparably profitable circumstances. Proponents of the measure said that it would provide revenue and savings for the government and relieve the people of certain burdens imposed by the old system of collection.

3. *Farming Loans.* Loans were made available to farmers, who were to repay the loans at 2 per cent monthly interest. The purpose was said to be to free farmers of the depredations of money-lenders, who charged much higher rates of interest. Wang denied that profit to the government was a purpose and explained the interest charges as necessary to cover the cost of administration.

4. *Hired-Services System.* A graduated tax was levied on families to provide funds to hire men for work previously performed as obligatory service.

5. Pao-chia *System.* To reduce the size of the professional armed forces and to save money, able-bodied men, chosen in turn from groups of households, were called up for local training and military duty. The groups of households (*pao*) also bore collective responsibility for individuals of a group.

6. *Reformed Examinations.* Together with a number of changes in state schools, Wang revised the civil service examinations to put more stress on issues of judgment, the "general meaning" of the classics, and matters of government and less on poetry and lyrical prose.

The question whether Wang was a practical reformer has been part of the discussion about him ever since he became chief councillor. The question has been asked, at least implicitly, in two senses. In the more technical sense, it may mean, were the measures that Wang An-shih devised likely to change conditions as he wanted them changed? In a more "political" sense, it could mean, did Wang An-shih behave in the ways best suited to win acceptance of his program? To answer the question in the first sense became more difficult than it might have been when Wang, after only about seven years as councillor, lost power, and a few years later opponents of the program altered much of it. Changes that a longer enforcement of the program would have brought became thereafter a matter of speculation. Even during the period of the New Laws, however, men were arguing that Wang's devices were wrong and would lead—in fact were already leading—to evils greater than the faults that needed correcting. In the second sense, the outcome of the experiment could be cited in support of the simple answer, "No": the way that Wang acted won little support for his efforts. His stubbornness, lack of tact, and short temper were qualities least likely to promote the political atmosphere of cooperation that might make broad reforms possible. The hostility Wang provoked among influential men and the reaction that followed his fall point to the impractical nature, politically speaking, of Wang's behavior. Even so, there have been those who argue that Wang faced a hostile majority of officials who feared changes such as he proposed and could not be moved by either argument or diplomacy. The inference to be drawn from this argument seems to be that Wang did the best that could be done against overwhelming opposition.

However that may be, few men have been able to separate the technical aspect from the personal one when they consider the period. Wang as a man has almost invariably colored discussion of the New Laws. For Chinese of the old school it is understandably so. The relation of virtue in a man to success in his government was so close that there could hardly be one without the other. It was natural that criticism of unusual measures designed by a man of unusual character seemed to demand examination of the man as well as his works. Where Wang and his works were concerned, men of his time expressed an excitement that marked the experience

as one of the most moving in Chinese history.

The second group of readings in this book represents responses to Wang and his program by men of his own time. One kind of response was to attack Wang directly. Lü Hui, in accusing Wang of pride, opportunism, egotism, nepotism, factionalism, arrogation of authority, willfulness, and dictatorial ambitions, was more restrained than some. At least he did not dwell on Wang's slovenly appearance. Another kind of response was one made by Su Shih, who attempted to criticize some of the New Laws as leading to economic and social disruption. In doing so, Su Shih placed his argument within a great traditional theme: the virtue of the ruler, as measured by the hearts of men, would be betrayed by imposing intolerable hardship on men. Ssu-ma Kuang, the towering historian and a leader of the opposition to Wang, showed in some of his statements that he was not blind to Wang's abilities. In the selection given here, however, he charges that Wang's ambition and arrogance led him to devise measures which, far from improving conditions, oppressed the people and encouraged misgovernment among officials.

After Wang's death, a desire began to be felt to assess the man in retrospect. Two great philosophers of the Southern Sung period (1127–1279), writing about three generations after the period of reform, attempted to see Wang as his impassioned contemporaries could not, and to show that a figure so great must have many parts. Lu Hsiang-shan, though he would not endorse everything Wang proposed, insisted that Wang's sincerity and purpose were beyond reproach. However, it was with an excessive determination that he had pursued his purpose, driving other great men who opposed him from the Court and opening the way to crafty self-seekers. This had been his greatest fault. Lu found little that was noble in the opposition to Wang and, what was perhaps worse, nothing constructive. The opposition, he charged, must share blame for wrongs done in the name of reform, since they had never based their complaints clearly on reason. Chu Hsi agreed with Lu Hsiang-shan's opinion of Wang's character. He pointed out that reform had been the goal and plan of many statesmen of the time, including some who later opposed Wang. In sensing that Wang's famous stubbornness was in part a product of the opposition he increasingly encountered, Chu suggested how the conflicts of the time must have affected the character of the men.

Writers of modern times have, with some exceptions, approached Wang's regime more or less in the first of our meanings, inquiring whether Wang's plans promised to improve the state of affairs in China. Writers have also tended to judge Wang in terms of modern political and economic attitudes, especially their own. Thus for J. C. Ferguson, writing early in the twentieth century, Wang was an admirably utilitarian, socialistic reformer with an intense sympathy for the people and anxiety for their welfare. Some thirty years later, H. R. Williamson, in the most extensive study of Wang An-shih in English, defended almost the whole of Wang's program, as designed to repress the rich and aid the poor, as practicable (if only it had been given enough time), and even as politically feasible (if the opposition had been wise enough to put up with Wang's idiosyncracies).

An opposite position, in some ways modern and in others close to traditional Chinese criticism of Wang, was taken by Lin Yutang. Despite his effort not to base judgment on the motives of the men involved, he gave great weight to personal character in his condemnation of Wang, as had Sung dynasty critics. In his view of the New Laws, the consideration of freedom was a basic issue, an issue which evokes the modern West more than eleventh-century China.

One line of inquiry common to many modern studies of Wang, the influence of social and economic class on the actions of men of the time, held a dogmatic position for Teng Kuang-ming. The selection here is not an analysis of Wang's reforms themselves but a statement of the thesis within which Wang's regime must be explained. In general the outlines of his thesis follow a Communist approach to society and history: the existence of a state of hostility or warfare between the exploiting or governing class and the exploited classes, the preoccupation of the exploiters with repressing the exploited, and the dictation of individual behavior by class interest. There is evidence in his essay, such as his obvious interest in Wang An-shih as a great man, of a historian's fascination with personalities. It might seem that in a fuller development of his subject he would pay more attention to the interplay of individuals and ideas than the Marxist law of class warfare ordinarily suggests. Yet the law will be observed. He obscures the fact that Ssu-ma Kuang and others admitted a need for reform and simplifies their attitude to one of complete hostility, indicating that individual attitudes, even if they seem to contradict the thesis, will not be permitted to refute it. The general setting of his conclusions seems predictable. Wang An-shih, at best a reformer, unable by reason of his class interests to accept a proletarian revolution, could never have done enough. History, impelled by impersonal forces of class interests, would roll on.

Ichisada Miyazaki attempts, on the basis of a comprehensive reading of the sources, to do more than recapitulate the elements of the reforms and the reactions to them. He is concerned to establish clearly the major emphases of the events and to fit the period into the course of Chinese history in more significant terms. Accepting the influence of class interests as important in social events, he also sees great men, group feelings, and personal relationships as forces in history. His general conclusion, that the weight of ingrained practices eventually subverted Wang's program, should not obscure the implication throughout the essay that, despite serious mistakes that probably brand Wang as "impractical," he was a brilliant figure on the right track.

James T. C. Liu's contribution to the growing appreciation of Wang An-shih has been mainly in analysis, both of what Wang aimed to do and of factors of Chinese civilization affecting his efforts. In the selections here, Liu applies to the situation of the time categories and concepts of modern political analysis, adapted to the characteristics of the Chinese state. He finds Wang an idealist who hoped to use the principal institution of China, the bureaucracy, to create a moral society in Confucian terms. Wang's failure, he suggests, could be blamed partly on the impracticality of his reforms in a certain objective sense—one or another of his policies gave grounds for complaint to almost all important groups of society and won the unswerving support of none of them—and partly on his impracticality as a politician, in that he failed to win the strong loyalty of any important group of the bureaucracy. The conclusion brings us back, no doubt, to the original question, but, let us hope, with a greater perception of what the event meant than was possible at the beginning.

NOTE ON CHINESE NAMES

The spelling of Chinese names varies in the following selections. Where the identity of the figure was apt to be in doubt, the editor has revised the spelling according to the Wade-Giles system of romanization. In the selections from Williamson and Lin Yutang some of the variations are slight and do not alter the sound of the names much. These have not been changed. Thus, for example, the following spellings occur for the name of the same man:

Williamson	*Lin Yutang*	*Wade-Giles*
Shen Tsung	Shentsung	Shen-tsung
Lü Hui Ch'ing	Lu Huiching	Lü Hui-ch'ing
Wang An Shih	Wang Anshih	Wang An-shih

ALPHABETICAL LIST OF IMPORTANT MEN OF THE PERIOD

All the following men were officials of high enough rank to make their opinions known in the Court. Some changed their attitude toward Wang An-shih, most often from support to opposition, in the course of the period.

Chang Fang-p'ing (1007–1091)	Older official, opponent of Wang's advancement.
Chao Pien (1008–1084)	Early supporter of Wang An-shih, later opponent.
Cheng Hsia (1041–1119)	Student of Wang and early supporter, later opponent.
Ch'eng Hao (1032–1085)	Philosopher, advocate of reform, but opponent of Wang An-shih.
Fan Chen (1008–1088)	Friend of Ssu-ma Kuang, opponent of Wang An-shih.
Fan Ch'un-jen (1027–1101)	Opponent of Wang An-shih.
Fu Pi (1004–1083)	Respected elder statesman, active in earlier reforms.
Han Ch'i (1008–1075)	Respected elder statesman, active in earlier reforms.
Han Wei (1017–1098)	Former tutor of Emperor, early friend and supporter of Wang An-shih, later opponent.
Li Ting	Pupil of Wang An-shih and later supporter and associate.
Lü Hui	Censor, one of the first to publish attack on Wang.
Lü Hui-ch'ing (1031–1111)	Principal associate of Wang An-shih.
Lü Kung-chu (1018–1089)	Influential and early supporter of Wang, later opponent.
Ou-yang Hsiu (1007–1070)	Older official, supporter of reform, early patron of Wang An-shih, later opponent.
Shen-tsung (Reigned 1068–1085)	Emperor.
Ssu-ma Kuang (1019–1086)	Great historian, eventually principal opponent of Wang An-shih.
Su Ch'e (Su Tzu-yu) (1039–1112)	Opponent of Wang, brother of Su Shih.
Su Shih (Su Tung-p'o) (1036–1101)	Poet, calligrapher, opponent of Wang An-shih. Brother of Su Ch'e.
Tseng Kung-liang (999–1078)	Older councillor, early sponsor of Wang An-shih, later opponent.
Tseng Pu (1035–1107)	Principal associate of Wang An-shih.
Wang An-shih (1021–1086)	Powerful prime minister and reformer; classicist, essayist, poet.
Wang Yen-sou	Opponent of Wang An-shih.
Wen Yen-po (1006–1097)	Councillor, recommended Wang for special promotion; later opposed him.

The Conflict of Opinion

"This man was entrusted with the administration of government. His advice was acted upon, and his plans were followed. . . . He was self-satisfied and self-opinionated, considering himself without equal among the men of the past and present. He did not know how to select what was best in the laws and institutions of the imperial ancestors and to bring together the happiest proposals put forth throughout the empire, so as to guide the imperial intelligence and assist in accomplishing the great task. . . . All he wanted was to satisfy his own ambitions, without regard to the best interests of the nation."

—Ssu-ma Kuang

"For he was a man of heroic mould and will, entirely free from the love of luxury, vice, wealth, or even fame. He stood aloof from those who pursued a merely conventional policy in such matters. He was an outstanding example of moral purity and determination. And as for his ideal, his purpose was to sweep the country clean of merely conventional practices, and to eliminate every trace of the *laissez-faire* policy of those officials who either refused to recognize, or failed to see, the necessity for administrative reforms."

—Lu Hsiang-shan

". . . Wang An-shih was a man of deep thought and broad sympathies. He was of the utilitarian school but his heart was with the suffering populace. His moral enthusiasm never failed him in the face of hostile criticism, and he labored steadily for the good of the people. . . . Though he was practical, he still sought to conserve the good of the past which had been handed down but was anxious to develop and improve upon it."

—John C. Ferguson

"Ssu Ma Kuang criticized Wang An-shih as being of 'unpractical mind,' and as 'being unacquainted with practical affairs.' But the most cursory glance at the character of the various reform measures which he promoted is sufficient to disprove such assertions. He may not have given sufficient consideration to the fact that there were not enough highminded men in the government service to ensure the success of his different projects, or he may have overlooked the fact that as his measures in the main were directed against the wealthy and influential classes, they would raise such opposition that his measures must eventually fail to produce those permanent results which he expected. Or again he may not have given sufficient thought to the fact that some of his measures would interfere with the customary and easy-going ways of the common people. . . . If that is what Ssu Ma Kuang meant by his 'being impractical' or 'unacquainted with practical affairs' he may perhaps be considered justified in making the statements. But if he meant that Wang An-shih was ignorant of the need of his country, and lacked the ideas for meeting that need in practical fashion, his criticism is quite beside the mark."

—H. R. Williamson

"Wang An-shih was a curious man, extraordinary in mind and character. He was an industrious student, a good scholar except in his abominable philology, and certainly a major poet. Unfortunately, he combined a Messianic sense of mission with a deplorable lack of tact and inability to get along with anyone but himself. He was at the same time unquestionably an impractical idealist."

—Lin Yutang

"All the New Laws produced worthy effects. At the least, finances took a turn for the better. Social order was also improved. There are some writers who ascribe the fall of Northern Sung . . . to Wang An-shih; but what Chinese dynasty has not fallen? . . . But in China reforms have often been eaten away in concessions to the mode of things as they are. Good measures and splendid ideas have been eviscerated. It was extremely regrettable that . . . the original ideas were progressively watered down in practice. If there had never been Wang An-shih's reforms, who could have guaranteed that Sung's pulse would surely go on beating those last fifty years?"

—Ichisada Miyazaki

"In Wang's view the bureaucracy was especially important. Yet, precisely on this point he failed, for he did not obtain strong enough support from the bureaucrats. He did not even succeed in inspiring a sustaining loyalty among the executive type of bureaucrats, upon whom he depended principally to carry out the New Politics. . . . Wang was theoretical in policy matters rather than practical in politics. . . . Thus, though he emphasized the importance of the bureaucracy, he did not really carry the support of the bureaucracy at all."

—James T. C. Liu

WANG AN–SHIH'S APPROACH TO REFORM

The Ten Thousand Word Memorial

WANG AN-SHIH

This memorial was submitted to the Emperor Jen Tsung in the year 1058, when Wang An Shih returned to the capital from the district of Chiang-Tung, where he had been acting as Chief-Justice of the Circuit for one year.

I, your Majesty's ignorant and incapable servant, have been honored with your commission to take a part in the administration of one of the circuits. I feel it to be my duty, now that I am called to Court to report on conditions in my district, to bring to your attention certain matters affecting the Government. I presume to do this on the ground of the experience gained during my period of official service, and regardless of my own inability. I shall consider it most fortunate if my suggestions receive your careful attention, and if you can see your way to adopt such as seem in your opinion to be of a reasonable character.

Your Majesty is well known to be of a careful and economical disposition, endowed with great knowledge and wisdom, devoted and energetic in the discharge of your routine duties, and to be entirely averse to licentious and time-wasting pleasures. Your love for the people is cherished by all. Your method of selecting those whom people desire to be in the highest offices of the State, in a public manner, and your appointment of them regardless of the opposition of slanderous and speciously clever folk, has never been surpassed, not even by the rulers of the Golden Age.[1]

[1] i.e. the two emperors and three kings, by which are meant Yao, Shun, Yü, T'ang, and

When one bears these things in mind, it might naturally be expected that poverty would be unknown in any homestead, and that the Empire as a whole would be gloriously prosperous.

Such, however, is not the case. One cannot ignore the fact that the internal state of the country calls for most anxious thought, and that the pressure of hostile forces on the borders is a constant menace to our peace. The resources of the Empire are rapidly approaching exhaustion, and the public life is getting more and more decadent. Loyal and courageous hearts are becoming increasingly apprehensive as to the outcome of this unsatisfactory state of affairs.

My own opinion is that all this is the result of the prevailing ignorance of a proper method of government. I realize that against this may be urged the fact that the Imperial laws are being strictly enforced,

---

Wen-Wu, the last two being regarded as one, for Wen Wang never actually ruled as king . . . Yao and Shun belong to the prehistorical period, but are usually dated as 2357–2205 B.C. Yü initiated the Hsia Dynasty in 2205 B.C., T'ang the Shang or Yin Dynasty in 1766 B.C., and Wu Wang founded the Chow Dynasty in 1122 B.C. As model rulers they represent the traditional Golden Age of Chinese history, though the Dynasties they founded in each case ended up ingloriously.

From H. R. Williamson, *Wang An Shih,* London: Arthur Probsthain, 1935, 2 vols., I: 48–84 (including headnote). Reprinted by permission.

and that the regulations for the administration of affairs are quite adequate. My meaning, however, is not that we have no laws and regulations, but that the present system of administration is not in accordance with the principles and ideas of the ancient rulers.

We read in Mencius, "When a ruler is sincerely loving, and generally known to be so, but the effects of his benevolent disposition are not realized by the people in any adequate way, it must be because the method of government is not molded after the pattern of the ancient rulers." We need look no further than this quotation to discover the reason for the defective character of the extant administration.

I am not arguing that we should revive the ancient system of government in every detail. The most ignorant can see that a great interval of time separates us from those days, and our country has passed through so many vicissitudes since then that present conditions differ greatly. So a complete revival is practically impossible. I suggest that we should just follow the main ideas and general principles of these ancient rulers.

Let us recall the fact that we are separated from the rule of these great men by over a thousand years of history: that they had their periods of progress and decline: that their difficulties and circumstances differed greatly. But although the measures they devised and adopted to meet their various circumstances varied in character they were at one in the motives which actuated them, and in their observance of the relative importance of affairs.

Therefore I contend that we need only to follow their principles. I believe that if that could be done, the changes and reforms that would ensue would not unduly alarm the people, or excite undue opposition, but would in the end bring the government of our day into line with that of the Golden Age.

Though that is true, I am bound to admit that the present state of affairs is of such a character that even though your Majesty should desire to reform the administration it would be practically impossible to do so. It may be urged that as your Majesty is of such a careful and restrained disposition, your intelligence and wisdom, and your loving consideration for the people, are all that is necessary to success, provided that you devote yourself sincerely to the task. My reason for saying that the realization of your object is impossible is that there is an insufficient number of capable men to help you. Without these it is not feasible to reform the government so that it may conform to the pattern of that set up by the ancient rulers.

My observation leads me to suggest that there never has been such a scarcity of capable men as exists today in the service of the State. Should it be urged that these men do exist, but that they are hidden away in the country districts, I would say that although I have prosecuted my search with diligence, I have found very few indeed.

Does not this indicate that the method of producing such men is faulty? I may be permitted to quote my own experience of official life, for it adds weight to my impression that capable men are too scarce. In my travels through my Circuit, extending over 300 miles, I have found extremely few officials who are able to carry out government orders in any satisfactory way, or who have the capacity to lead their people to fulfil their obligations to the State. On the contrary those who are incapable, negligent, avaricious and mean, are innumerable. In some prefectures there is absolutely no one who is capable of applying the ideas of the ancient rulers to current conditions, or of even explaining how such might be done. The result is that no matter how fine and complete the regulations and orders of the Court might be, the possible benefit of these is never realized by the people because of the incapacity of the local officials. Not only is that true, but the subordinates in the districts are able to take advantage of these orders to carry on corrupt practices and induce disturbances. . . .

To my mind the greatest need of the time is the securing of capable officials. We should ensure that an increasing number of these should be made available for the services of the State, so that from this larger group we shall be able to select a sufficient number for our purpose, and secure the possibility of getting men into their right positions. Granted that, it should not be difficult, having due regard to time and circumstances, and acting always in accordance with the dictates of humanity and reason, to so reform the method of government administration that it will follow on the lines laid down by the ancient rulers.

Although the modern Empire is the same as that ruled by the ancients, there is this scarcity of capable men in the government services, while in their day such men were numerous. How are we to account for that? I believe it is due to our not having the right method of producing them.

During the Shang dynasty the Empire was in the greatest confusion. Those in office were covetous and corrupt, the harbingers of decay and disaster, for they were not the right men for their posts. At the time Wen Wang came forth, capable men for the administration were all too few. But he trained the people in such a way that this defect was soon made good. He had no shortage of capable administrators, and he was able to use them in positions for which they were fitted. As we read in the ode,

> Our joyous prince
> Can influence men.

His success is seen also from this:

> Even the rabbit catchers
> Are lovers of virtue.

If the rabbit catchers were of this character, we can be sure that those in government office were even more earnestly devoted to lofty ideals. It was because Wen Wang possessed this type of ability, that he induced submission of the foe whenever

he organized military expeditions, and that the country was well governed in times of peace. . . .

We infer from this that the number of capable men available depends upon the ruler taking such a course as shall develop these gifts in the people, and on making it possible for such to bring their natural gifts to fruition. By this I mean that a proper method should be devised whereby such men can be trained, maintained, selected and appointed.

Firstly, what is the proper method of instructing these?

The ancient rulers had a graded system of schools ranging from the National University to the district and village schools. For the control and development of these, a considerable number of educational officers and teachers were appointed, who had been selected with the greatest care. The conduct of Court ceremonies, music, and Government administration were all part of the recognized Curriculum. So that the model held up before the student, and in which he gradually became well versed, was the example, precept, and fundamental principles of government observed by the ancient rulers. The students trained under this system were found to be of such ability and character as the Government required and could use. No student was received into the schools who had not shown promise of developing such a capacity. But all who demonstrated that they possessed this potentiality were without exception received.

This I consider to be the right method of training these men.

Secondly, what is the proper method of maintaining them?

In a word, they should be given adequate financial provision; they should be taught the restraints of propriety, and controlled by adequate laws and regulations.

With regard to providing them with adequate financial resources, I would say that it is only natural for a man who is dissatisfied in this matter of financial provision, to proceed to all manner of loose and corrupt practices.

The ancient rulers were fully cognizant of this fact, and drew up their regulations governing salaries, beginning with those who were allocated a share in the public services, although not on the recognized official roll, ensuring that they received sufficient to make up for what they had lost by being called upon for public work, necessitating absence from their agricultural or other pursuits. In increasing scale the salaries advanced, assuring each official of whatever grade sufficient to keep him honest, self-respecting, and free from corruption. They then made further provision for the sons and grandchildren of officials by their system of maintenance grants. In these ways the ancient rulers ensured that the officials they employed had no undue anxieties during their own lifetime about the support of their families, or about exceptional expenditure such as was caused by weddings, funerals, and the entertainment of guests. They also so arranged matters that after their death their descendants should have no cause to grieve over an insufficiency of the means of life.

Then as regards the necessity of inculcating in them the restraints of propriety, I would say that once you have satisfied a man's natural desire for sufficient financial resources, it is essential that he should be restrained by the ordinances of propriety, otherwise he will proceed to a reckless extravagance in everything.

The ancient rulers were cognizant of this fact, and drew up a series of regulations regarding weddings, funerals, sacrifices, support of the aged, banquets, presents, dress, food, utensils, etc., etc. Expenditure on these things was to be regulated according to the rank and grade of official. The aim was to adjust their financial outlay in an equitable manner, having due regard to their varying circumstances. A man might have a certain rank, which, if that alone was considered, would demand the expenditure of considerable sums on

such things. But he might not possess the means to do the thing in the style which his rank required. The regulations provided for this contingency and he was not expected to conduct such matters in the lavish way that his rank alone would call for. But supposing a man had the means to meet all the requirements of high official rank on such occasions, but lacked the necessary rank which entitled him to make such a display, the regulations forbade him to do so, prohibiting the addition of the smallest fraction to the standard he was entitled to observe under them.

Further as regards the measures to be devised for controlling the officials.

The ancient rulers gave the officials moral instruction, as well as seeking to make them accomplished in the Arts. That having been done, those who failed to act up to the instruction they had received were banished to distant outposts, and were deprived of their official status for the whole of their life. They were also instructed in the restraints of Propriety. If they transgressed the rules in this sphere, the penalty exacted was banishment or even death.

We read in the Wang Chih section of the Li Chi, or Book of Rites, that if there was any delinquency committed in the matter of the proper clothing to be worn, that the prince of the State concerned should be banished.

In the Book of History in the section entitled "Chiu Kao" we read, "Should information come to you that drinking is going on, you should without delay proceed to arrest the drinkers, and bring them to the capital for execution."

It may be urged that such matters as wearing the wrong clothes or getting drunk are very light crimes, and that banishment or execution for the miscreants were altogether out of proportion. The fact that the ancient rulers permitted such heavy penalties was with a view to unifying the customs of the country, and thus accomplishing the true aim of all government.

By this imposition of the restraints of

Propriety and the penalties of the Law, they sought to bring all alike into subservience and submission. But they not only relied upon the power of prohibition and inspection, they afforded in their own person an example of sincere and sympathetic conduct. In this way all those officials of high rank who had direct access to the presence of the ruler, were induced to carry out his wishes in a loyal manner. It was agreed that punishment should be inflicted upon the one who failed to do so. The ruler gave a sincere example of living out his precepts, and those of high rank learned to avoid doing the things of which he disapproved. The idea was that thus the majority of the people at large would need no penalties to keep them from unworthy practices.

The above is the right method of maintaining the officials.

Thirdly, what is the correct method of selecting officials?

The method adopted by the ancient rulers was to permit the country folk and students in the village or district schools to recommend those whom they thought had the requisite character and ability for appointment by the throne. Investigation was then made as to the real character and ability of such men, and each was then given a period of probation in some position suited to his capacity.

It should be emphasized that in this investigation into the merits and ability of any candidate, personal observation or information from others were not the only factors on which the ruler depended. He never depended upon the judgment of any single individual either. A man's character was adjudicated by his conduct and his ability was tested by enquiry as to his views on current affairs. These having been ensured, he was actually tested out in some office for a time. As a matter of fact the meaning of the term "investigation" was just this period of probation in actual employment. Yao's appointment of Shun was of this type. We can legitimately infer that

this would be the procedure stringently followed in regard to other appointments.

Now when we consider the vast extent of the Empire, and the enormous number of positions that have to be filled, one gets some idea of the large number of men that are required. We must acknowledge also that the Emperor cannot possibly investigate the character and ability of each and every one individually. Neither can he lay this responsibility on any individual, or expect him in a day or two to conduct such enquiry as would enable him to adjudicate the merit or demerit of any.

So I propose that those whom you have already found by experience to be of good character and great ability, and to whom you have committed important responsibilities, should be entrusted with the task of selecting men of like qualifications. Also that these should be given an adequate period of probation in official life, after which they too should be allowed to make recommendations to the throne. When this has been done, and when the men recommended have been found to be worthy, rank, emoluments, and promotion should be conferred by way of reward.

Fourthly, what is the right method to be adopted regarding the appointment of officials?

The ancient rulers were cognizant of the fact that men differ in character, and their ability for actual work. They recognized that they were specially suited for certain definite tasks, and could not be reasonably expected to take up any and every kind of work indiscriminately.

So they appointed those who had special qualifications for the work of Agriculture to the Ministry of Agriculture (like Hou Chi). Those who were skilled in engineering they appointed to the Ministry of Works (like Kung Kung). The chief positions were reserved for those who had the finest character and greatest ability, those of lesser gifts and qualifications being appointed to subordinate posts.

They further recognized the fact that it

is only after a prolonged period in any one appointment, allowing one's superior sufficient time to learn of his real capacity and attainments, and for the people under him to become truly subservient and happy under his control, that the really worthy have the chance to display their worth, and on the other hand that the evil-minded may have their wickedness exposed.

Hence they made provision for a prolonged period of probation, as the best method of testing the appointees. This being ensured, those of real character and ability realized that they would be afforded a full chance to carry their projects to a successful issue, and were not distressed by the prospect that possibly they could not carry out their ideas properly, or that they would be deprived of their just reward. On the other hand, idlers and negligent fellows, who have become inured to thinking that they might maintain their good name and position for a short time, would be stimulated to a more worthy view of their responsibilities, as they would be made aware of the certainty of degradation and disgrace which would ensue on a prolonged period of service, unless they reformed. Those who knew they possessed no ability for a certain post would refrain from assuming such on the same grounds.

After a prolonged period of probation in any one appointment, one's incapacity or unworthiness to occupy it, would certainly be manifest. This we have seen would deter unworthy or incapable men from embarking upon an official career. Still less would fawning and flattering folk find any inducement to compete for official position with this system functioning.

So we see that due caution was paid to the selection of officials in those days, that they were given appointments for which they were deemed qualified, that they were kept in office for a sufficiently lengthy period, that they were regulated and rewarded in a most careful manner, and were given freedom and authority for the proper discharge of their duties. They were not hedged about by a minutiæ of regulations and prohibitions, but were afforded a full opportunity for the carrying out of their own ideas.

The method adopted by Yao and Shun was of this order. In the Book of History we read, "There was an inspection of the record of officials once every three years. After three inspections of this type, promotion and fame, or degradation and disgrace were definitely decided upon." This quotation is apropos of my argument. In the times of Yao and Shun everyone knows whom they degraded, viz. the four villains, while the men they promoted and maintained in high office for the whole of life were the three worthy ones. Promotion meant the conferring of higher rank and the increase of their emoluments.

That then is the correct method of appointing officials.

The above represents what was the method in vogue in those days concerning the instruction, maintenance, selection and appointment of officials. The ruler availed himself to the full of the experience and advice of his great officers. By their joint help in seriously thinking of the best way of doing things, they were enabled to put this method into effect. As there was no suspicion between ruler and minister, they were enabled to carry out what they desired in the matter of government administration.

[*The following represents Wang An-shih's criticism of current practices in regard to the main topics already raised and his suggestions for reform.*]

I. *With regard to the method of instruction*

It is true that nowadays each "chow" and "hsien" is supposed to have schools. In reality, however, these schools are just so much "bricks and mortar." For there are no teachers or real training carried on in them. It is true there are instructors in the National University, but these are not selected with any care. Court ceremonies, music and government administration have no place in the curriculum. I admit that the students have a vague idea that these things form part of the responsibility of those in public office, but they do not apprehend that these are the very things with which they ought to make themselves fully acquainted.

In the main the instruction they receive consists of explanations of the texts of the Classics, analysed into sections and sentences. That, however, was not the ancient method.

More recently a new method of instructing students to prepare for the official tests by writing essays has come into existence. This method, however, calls for the recitation and memorizing of an enormous amount of literature, and the candidate must devote himself strenuously to this task the whole day long if he is to achieve success. But even if success in this matter is gained, it does not qualify the best student for the ruler's position, or the less successful for the other public services. So that even if they should go on learning in these schools until their hair turned grey, and give themselves the whole day long to the attempt to conform to the requirements of their superiors, they would have only the vaguest notion of what to do when they were appointed to actual office.

Not only does the present method of instruction fail to produce the type of man that is required, it actually spoils them so that they cannot become capable administrators. A man's capacity for government is best educed by specialization, and ruined by too great a variety of subjects to be studied. So we find that the ancient rulers in their search for capable men went to the factories for their artisans, to the farms for their agriculturists, to the markets for their commercial men, and to the schools for their officials. Each man thus had the opportunity of specializing in his own line, and was not compelled to study anything extraneous to the actual task of preparation for a particular job. It was felt that to do otherwise would be detrimental to the gaining of the specialized knowledge required. The scholars were also prohibited from studying anything other than the methods and principles of the ancient rulers, the various heterodox ideas of the different schools being banned under strict penalty.

The students of the present day ought to study methods of practical administration. But either no instruction at all is given, or they have to exhaust themselves in strenuous cultivation of the art of essay writing. The ancients gave their time and energy specifically to the study of practical administration, and yet not all developed equal ability for the same. But nowadays the time and energy of students is diverted into quite other channels, and they give themselves to useless studies. It is not to be wondered at that when such men are given government appointment very few find themselves capable of discharging their duties. . . .

Further, in the times of the ancient rulers, the students were given instruction in both civil and military subjects. It was also recognized that amongst the students there would be found some who had the capacity for high office, but that there would be others who would be suitable for only small posts. There was recognition of the fact that men differed in capacity, and also in their suitability for different kinds of work. In connection with the Military services, none who had not been specially trained in such matters were given positions, though those who had received such training were all given positions according to their ability. The better qualified were appointed to the chief civil posts during peace, or to the chief military posts in a time of border trouble or war. Those of lesser qualifications were appointed to the headship of the various civil groups, or to the command of the different military units. In this way the big Garrison posts, and the important Circuit positions were all filled by great men, who were at one and the same time both scholars and generals.

Nowadays great emphasis is laid upon

the distinction between civil and military matters by the students. The rule is that they confess to knowing nothing about military matters, being solely concerned with the civil services. So it comes about that important military positions are left to those who are termed "military men." These are often promoted from the hired levies, who in the main are the good-for-nothings of the country-side. For any who have the ability to maintain themselves alive in their own village are unwilling to offer themselves to the army. But these Garrison posts and other military commands are of the most vital importance to the country, and the selection of the right men for these positions ought to have the serious attention of the ruler. . . .

II. *With regard to the maintenance of officials*

The rate of salaries paid nowadays to officials is too low. With the exception of the very highly placed officials in the Court circle, all who have large families to support, engage either in agriculture or trade to eke out. Those in the lower positions like district officials are at the most in receipt of 8,000 or 9,000 "cash," while many only get as much as 4,000 or 5,000 a month. When the time during which they have to wait for appointments, and the intervals between appointments are taken into account, say over a period of six or seven years, we find that they only receive the equivalent of three years' allowances. So that they draw in actual cash an average of less than 4,000 or 5,000 "cash" a month. From this they have to provide the wages of a servant, and make provision for the support of their parents; and funeral and wedding expenses.

It may be urged that a man of superior character will maintain his integrity and good name, even though he should be in very poor circumstances financially. It is also commonly said that a man of inferior moral character will remain mean even though he should become rich. But the mediocre man does not come within these general rules. In this case poverty induces moral degradation, and wealth helps him to maintain his good name. If we consider for a moment the whole of the educated class in the country, not more than 1 per cent may be classed as either superior or inferior men. Practically all are of the mediocre class, in whom, as I have just said, poverty induces moral degradation, and wealth helps to maintain their good name.

The ancient rulers were cognizant of the fact that the great majority could not be compelled by force to adopt any line of action, and so adopted the mediocre man and not themselves as their standard. So they sought to lead men along the lines of their natural inclination, with the idea that by the adoption of a method which the ordinary man could observe and practice, they might be able to carry out their ideas for the empire, and ensure permanence for them.

With the present scale of salaries, however, it is impossible for the ordinary man to be honest and self-respecting, and it is useless to expect that he should. So we find that the big officials both offer and receive bribes and presents, and carry on private business, thinking nothing of being regarded as "corrupt." The smaller fry of the official world practice all manner of device for making money, not only engaging in trade and barter, but even descending to begging. Once the officials have earned the reputation of being corrupt, they become negligent, caring for nothing but the holding of their positions. Real earnestness and devotion to the public cause become unknown. With official duties neglected in this fashion, it is of course impossible for government to make any sound progress. But when bribery is added, and intimidation with a view to "mulcting" the people, we see the implication of the statement that we are not providing our officials with sufficient financial help.

Again, seeing that there are no regulations controlling expenditure on weddings, funerals, support of parents, clothes, food, and the appurtenances of life, everyone comes to regard extravagance as admirable, and economy as disgraceful. If a man has wealth he does everything in the most lavish style, merely following the line of his own fancy. As this is in no way prohibited by the authorities, the people begin to look upon it as the right thing to do. A man who is of straitened means, and who cannot live up to this conventional standard of doing things, constantly offends his relatives in such matters as weddings and funerals. So men are led to regard economy as something to be ashamed of. The wealthy seek for more wealth and become completely addicted to the lust for money, while the poor with their limited means exhaust their resources in the attempt to "keep up" with them. It thus becomes doubly difficult for an official to be honest. . . .

I know that the law in these days is particularly severe against avaricious practices by the officials. But on the one hand to issue such prohibitions, and at the same time to disregard extravagance and waste, is to lay the emphasis in the wrong place, regarding the non-essential as important, and disregarding that which is absolutely fundamental.

One of the main criticisms of the present administration is that supernumerary officials are too many, especially considering the straitened condition of the exchequer. It is true that the number of officials engaged is extremely large, but even when they were fewer and salaries small, the national Treasury was still short of funds. The matter of official salaries is a comparatively negligible factor anyhow.

I have made no special study of the subject of finance, but I have made some enquiry into the methods of finance adopted by the ancient rulers. In a word, this consisted of using the resources of the people to produce wealth for the State, and to devote the wealth thus accumulated to meeting the requirements of the national expenditure. In those times we find they never experienced stringency in the national exchequer. But they did consider it calamitous not to make use of an efficient method of finance.

At the present time we have no preparations for war on our hands; the people are peacefully pursuing their various avocations, and are doing their utmost to produce wealth for the State. Yet we are constantly distressed by the prevailing financial stringency both in regard to the national Treasury and the people generally. The reason must lie in the fact that we have not secured the right method of administering the State finances, and that the authorities are unable to devise appropriate measures to meet the situation. Once the proper method is secured, and the necessary reforms made, I am sure, even though I may be considered stupid, that official salaries may be raised without causing the financial condition of the country to be adversely affected.

It may be urged that the laws and regulations for the inspection and control of the officials are both strict and adequate. But in the ethical instruction which we have given them, one would like to enquire whether they have been sufficiently enlightened concerning the punishments attendant upon their non-observance of the rules laid down. The same with regard to our efforts to restrain them by the rules of propriety, and in giving them their official charge. They should have been fully warned about the penalties for disobedience. Unless this preliminary work of admonition has been duly carried out, it would be wrong to inflict punishments in case of disobedience or transgression. The ancient rulers made these three features a matter of the greatest concern.

Nowadays officials cannot be punished, because they have not had this preliminary tuition in admonition and warning. The procedure is of another kind. A multitude of trifling prohibitions hedge them about, and these are constantly being altered. They are so numerous and so detailed that the officials cannot even keep a record of them. So one need not point out that it is practically impossible not to offend in some cases. This is one of the great reasons why the laws and regulations of the Government are trifled with, and fail to be effective. For as things stand, it is quite possible that a veritable scoundrel might have the good luck to avoid incurring penalties, while the really loyal and good official might have the misfortune to get himself involved. This is what is involved in our inability to control the officials by the laws, and is one of the results of our failure to secure the right method of maintaining them.

III. *With regard to the method of selection of officials*

The present method of selecting officials is as follows: If a man has a colossal memory, can repeat extensive portions of the classics, and has some skill at composition, he is termed specially brilliant or worthy, and chosen for the highest grades of State ministers. Those who are not possessed of such retentive memories, or of such wide recitative powers, and yet have some skill in composition, showing their gifts of poesy and rhyming, are granted the "Chin Shih" degree, the highest of which are also eligible to be appointed to the high positions. It should need no discussion to show that the knowledge and skill which these men display in no sense of itself fits them for such places of authority and distinction. It is, however, the prevailing opinion, that this method which has been used so long has been proved capable of producing men suitable for these posts. It is then urged that it is quite unnecessary to alter the regulations, or to seek to follow the ancient practice in the matter. That I contend is faulty reasoning.

Under the regime of the ancient rulers, although they most carefully observed the proper method of selecting their officials, they continued to be apprehensive lest the really worthy should in any way be hindered from gaining access to the highest positions in the land, and lest the unworthy should get mixed up with their betters. Nowadays when the ancient method is rejected, men of mere literary ability are regarded as worthy and efficient, as capable of fulfilling the responsibilities of the highest office, and it is considered quite right that such men should be appointed thereto.

It is of course reasonable to assume that some men of literary ability should prove themselves equal to carrying the responsibilities of high office, but mere literary skill should not be the only factor to be taken into account, for on that score unworthy men might also be elected to these responsible positions. As a matter of fact nine out of every ten who are capable of administering the duties of these high positions have spent their lives in subordinate posts in the provinces, just because they did not possess the necessary literary ability, which as I have said, is of itself no real help to a man occupying an administrative position. . . .

One other basis of selection is a man's knowledge of the Nine classics, or the Five classics, or a special knowledge of One classic, or again on his knowledge of Law subjects. The Court has already realized that this knowledge is of no value for practical administrators, and has made certain modifications in the old system, requiring more a knowledge of the general ideas of the Classics. The men gained by this change are really no improvement on those gained by the old method. So a further modification was made later requiring men to understand the general classical ideas with a view to promoting those who were skilled in classical interpretation and practical applications. But these changes are of little value. For those who get selected by this method are still those of colossal memories and skill in composition. Those who really understand the ideas of the ancient rulers, and who are capable of applying them in a practical manner to government problems are not of necessity to be gained by this procedure.

Still another type of official gets his appointment out of sheer favoritism. These are mainly the sons or brothers of those already in the government service. They have neither received any instruction in the schools, nor have they been examined by the authorities as to their ability. Many are those whom their own brothers or fathers cannot guarantee as to their morals. Yet they receive the commission of the Court and are granted both rank and office.

Wu Wang in recounting the crimes of Chow included the following: "He appointed men to office on the hereditary principle." He meant to indicate by this that the appointment of officials on the hereditary principle, without regard to a man's ability or character, was the reason why Chow threw the country into confusion and eventually brought his dynasty to ruin. On that ground later rulers who achieved success in their administration refrained from adopting the method.

There is still another set of officials to whom I should refer, namely the "unclassed." The Court has already indicated by their designation that they are lacking in conscientious scruples, and limited their possibilities of promotion. That is as it should be so far. But these men are employed in subordinate posts in the districts, and this gives them a standing above that of the ordinary person. This can hardly be considered an observance of the dictum that "the worthy should rule the unworthy." From my own practical observation of officials over a large area, I find that there are many officials functioning who are of this "unclassed" type. But I know only two or three all told who are capable of assuming responsibility for affairs, and these without exception need to be closely watched lest they proceed to all manner of illegal practices. . . .

IV. *With regard to the appointment of officials*

I have already indicated that the current method of selecting officials is wrong in principle. I have now to add that in the actual appointing of a man to office, no enquiry is made as to his real capability for the particular post to which he is allocated. All that is considered is his year of graduation, or his particular position in the examination lists. Or again instead of investigating his suitability for a certain position, regard is paid only to the number of years he has been engaged in the government service.

On the basis of possessing literary ability a man may be appointed to a Financial post, then he may be transferred to a legal position, or again to an office connected with the Board of Rites. One cannot expect anything else than that he finds it difficult to fill any office in any satisfactory manner, seeing that he is required to be ready to fill any position whatsoever. It is only natural in such circumstances to find very few who can fulfil their obligations in any one position. That had led in its turn to their falling into the habit of doing nothing at all. If a man receives an appointment to the Board of Rites, he is in nowise concerned about his utter ignorance of Rites, for the simple reason that he knows that those in the Rites department have never received any instruction in the business of their office. The same holds true with regard to those appointed to the legal positions. . . .

Then I must refer to the current practice of frequent transfer of officials from one place to another. The fact that men are not allowed to remain in one office for any length of time prevents their superiors from getting to know them or their ability in any real sense. Again, those in inferior positions, because they have not had time to learn to respect superiors, are mostly unwilling to obey them. A worthy man has not sufficient time to bring his plans to fruition, and an unworthy man does not remain long enough in any one post for his evil disposition to manifest itself. There are other evils attendant upon this system, such as the burden which devolves upon the local population in the constant receptions of new officials, and the farewells to old occupants of the positions. There are too many defects in accounting and the keeping of records for which these constant changes are responsible. These are among the minor evils attendant upon this system.

It ought to be a rule that appointments should be made for a protracted period, relatively longer periods being allowed to those who have control of greater areas, or particularly heavy responsibilities. Only in that case can we expect a man to make some really valuable and constructive contribution to the state. But the current practice is of a contrary type, many officials being transferred after only a few days in one post.

There are then these defects in regard to the government system. No care is exercised in the selection of officials, and they are appointed to positions regardless of their fitness or otherwise for them. Officials are not allowed to remain in any one post long enough to make any effective contribution.

Another defect I must now stress is that after they are appointed to office, they are not trusted to carry out their duties. An official is hedged about by a multitude of minute prohibitions and hindrances, so that he simply cannot carry out any ideas he may chance to have. This is one of the great reasons why those now in the government service are mainly unsuited for their positions. Since you have the wrong men in office I realize that unless you should hedge them about in this way, they would proceed to all manner of lawlessness if given the slightest liberty. That may be true. But what I wish particularly now to emphasize is that history proves it to be impossible to secure proper government by merely relying on the power of the law to control officials when the latter are not the right men for their job. It is equally futile to expect efficient government if, having the right men in their proper positions, you hedge them about by a multitude of minute and harassing prohibitions.

Seeing that all the evils outlined above do exist, even though worthy and able men should find their way into the government service, it is just as if they were unworthy and incapable. . . .

But the shortage of men of capacity in office, and the impossibility of reviving the method of government adopted by the ancient rulers, on that account, are not the only evils.

The military situation, and the safety of the country are involved. We cannot expect a continuation of past good fortune in this respect such as might free your Majesty from every cause for anxiety.

We have before us the instance of Chang Chueh of the Han dynasty. With 360,000 men he rebelled, as it were in a single day. There was no one within his state able to forestall him. We remember too the revolt of Huang Ch'ao of the T'ang dynasty, who brought about a general uprising, and marched unopposed by either civil or military official, right through the land. The ruin of Han and the downfall of T'ang can be traced to these two sources.

After the downfall of T'ang, there was gradual deterioration through the period of the Five Dynasties. Then the military men were in power, and all the worthy men retired into private life. It seemed as though they had completely disappeared in fact. Those in power then ceased to pay any attention to the rightful distinction between ruler and official, between superior and subordinate. In those days it was as easy to change the dynasty as it was to make a move in a game of chess. The corpses of the people littered the field, and they considered it most fortunate if they escaped with their lives. Disasters of that type are brought about by the absence of capable men in office.

I am greatly concerned that at present, among your Majesty's high ministers and officers, there are none who are exercising any forethought on your behalf, or who are planning for the permanence of the Dynasty.

Let us recall the fact that Chin Wu Ti lived entirely in the present and made no plans for the welfare of his descendants. Let us remember that during his time, those who held office under him, were mere timeservers and menpleasers: that the public life was utterly corrupt: that the usual observances of propriety were spurned: the laws utterly ignored, and that officials and people alike had no conscience at all on these great matters. Anyone with the least intelligence could foresee that it would result in disaster. This at length came upon them; there was utter confusion throughout the land, and for over two hundred years China was in the grip of barbarian tribes.

I think with the gravest concern of your Majesty's responsibilities in being entrusted with the care of this great empire by the spirits of your ancestors. Their hope is that it shall persist for endless generations, and that the millions of your people will never know the pinch of poverty or the menace of invasion. I implore your Majesty to note the reason for the fall of Han and T'ang and the confusion and decadence of the Five Dynasties, and to take warning from the calamity which overtook Chin Wu Ti for his negligence and *laissez-faire* policy.

I trust too that you will make it quite clear to your ministers that they should take steps to ensure the production of capable men, and that they may make such plans for this object as may be gradually carried into effect, seeking to adapt them to present circumstances, without doing violence to the principles of the ancient rulers. If such plans are made and rendered effective, the capable men will be more numerous than can be employed; you will have no desire which cannot be fulfilled, and there will be nothing that you cannot accomplish.

When I first began to study Mencius, and read that he said "It is easy to carry out the government of the ancient rulers," I thought that that was really so. But later on when I came to the place where Mencius was discussing with Shen Tzu about the territory of Ch'i and Lu, I realized that the area governed by the ancient rulers was generally speaking only about 100 li square. Then I began to see that if a new ruler were to arise he must induce the princes who were controlling territory of 1,000 li or 500 li in extent to reduce their area to some tens of li square. I began to doubt whether Mencius, worthy and wise though

he was, with wisdom and love so great that he could unify the whole empire, could without military force speedily reduce the territory of these princes by 80 or 90 per cent so that they should revert to the conditions which obtained in the days of the ancient rulers.

Later on again I began to take thought about the policy of Chu Fu Yen of which Han Wu Ti availed himself. His plan was to order the princes of states and rulers of territories to apportion as gifts of grace parts of their territory to their sons. At the same time the emperor fixed the titles and designations of these, bringing them all under the direct control of the ruler. In this way the territory got split up into smaller regions, the sons and brothers of the princes each getting their own share. But the plan ultimately resulted in the powerful and great princes being deprived of much of their influence, their large domains being split up into many smaller and weaker ones.

Thus I came to see that by careful planning and estimating, and making the changes gradually, the large could be made small, and the strong weak, without revolts or rebellions, or the confusion and distress of war. The words of Mencius were seen after all not to be either extravagant or unreasonable. So to my mind it became clear that the difficulties in the way of one wishing to introduce such changes were not so formidable as might at first sight appear. So I repeat we should plan carefully for the changes that need to be made, estimate everything, and gradually introduce the changes. Then it will be comparatively easy to carry them out.

But under the regime of the ancient rulers they were not so much concerned at what men left undone, as that they lacked the ability to do any particular thing. Again they were more concerned about their own inability to do things, or to get the people to do things, than they were about the people's inability to do them.

What man naturally desires is to live well, earn a good reputation, gain honourable rank, and get good pay. The success which attended the efforts of the ancient rulers in training the people to become their officers, and in gaining the loyal obedience of their officials so that good government was made to prevail, was entirely due to their giving them what they desired. When an officer found himself incapable of discharging the duties of any post, he gave it up. But granted that he had the ability, he exerted himself to make himself still more capable, and naturally would not resign the chance of getting what he really desired. That is the implication of my first point above.

By the second I mean that it was the practice of the ancient rulers to treat their officers handsomely, so that all who had any intelligence and ability at all, were enabled to make good progress. But it was considered vital that the emperor himself should give them an example of sincerity, and care, and devotion. This was with the idea that all might be stimulated to respond in a similar manner. So I say that their first concern was to rouse themselves to the task, rather than to be distressed at the inability of others.

If your Majesty is sincerely desirous of securing a body of capable officials to help you, and I believe you possess this desire, all that is necessary is that you should devote yourself to the task.

I have, however, observed that on former occasions whenever the Court has been desirous of introducing some reforms, that the pros and cons are most carefully considered at the beginning. But should some compromising and opportunist sort of fellow criticize the measure and evince some displeasure with it, the Court immediately desists and dare not go on with the matter.

The laws are not set up for the advantage of any one special class. Under the regime of the ancient rulers, their laws were administered for the whole empire and its benefit. But we must bear in mind that their regime was instituted after a time of corruption and decay, when it was considered most fortunate that such laws could be instituted at all. If after setting up their

laws, all the opportunists had been pleased to agree to their promulgation and there had been no opposition, then of course the laws of the ancient rulers would still have been extant.

However, not only were the times most difficult for the setting up of the laws, but the opportunist officials were all unwilling to carry them out, so whenever the ancient rulers desired to carry anything of importance into effect, they had to have recourse to punishments. Only then could they carry out their original ideas.

So we read in the Ode "Huang I"

By punishments and extermination,
We eliminate opposition.

The reference here is to the way in which Wen Wang carried out his ideas in the stabilizing of the empire. We find therefore that the ancient rulers, in their attempt to reform corrupt customs, and to create a body of capable officials, made their laws and regulations with firmness, and nerved themselves to the task even though they had to mete out strict punishments. They saw that there was no other way of carrying their plans through.

Think for a moment of Confucius, who though a commoner by birth, travelled to all the states, giving advice to the princes, causing them to relinquish old practices; to oppose what they had once approved; and succeeded in rousing them to attempt tasks which they had formerly despised. Yet with all his energy and devotion, he was greatly hampered ultimately by their opposition. That, however, in no sense dissuaded him from his purpose, as he knew perseverance was the only way to ensure success. In his determination he may be classed with Wen Wang.

Wen Wang is the greatest of all rulers, and Confucius the greatest of all sages. It is reasonable to suggest that all who are desirous of introducing reforms should act after their fashion. You exercise the power of regal sway, and occupy the throne of the ancient rulers. You have not the difficulty that they had in regard to this matter of punishment. There are some opportunists who show their displeasure by criticizing and opposing anything in the nature of reform, but they are nothing like so numerous as those who will be delighted with and approve of such a policy.

You will therefore be at fault if you refrain from your purpose because of the displeasure or opposition of this conventional and opportunist body of opinion. If your Majesty is sincere in your desire to create a body of capable officials, I beseech you to tie yourself down to it absolutely. If in addition to having a policy of reform, you have the mind and will to carry out the same, gradually it may be, but nevertheless determinedly, you will be assured of success in your object, as far as I can see.

Unfortunately, it has to be admitted that these matters which I present to your notice are not the subjects which these conventionalists discuss. Those who are regarded as critics of current events either regard them as impracticable, or so commonplace as to be beneath their notice. I know that there are amongst your great officers those who are exerting themselves to the limit of their power and intelligence to assist you. But in the main their ideas are confined to the detailed discussion of any proposal that is made, and it is this power of discussion which is held in esteem as a practical gift. The great officials regard such a gift as of the most estimable and rare variety, and so naturally enough, the Court is guided by such considerations in the selection of their officials.

But they rarely or never touch upon those greater matters affecting human relationships, the laws of the land, the greater ceremonies and duties, the very things to which the ancient rulers devoted themselves so earnestly to understand and preserve. The moment anyone should raise discussion on any of these matters, the crowd begins to mock him as an unpractical idealist. . . .

Thus I have taken the opportunity of reporting on the affairs of my office, to discuss with you matters vital to the State. I have been outspoken regardless of my own incapacity. I have ventured to assert that there is a dearth of capable men in the public service, and that there are none who are capable of carrying out the ideas which your Majesty had in appointing them. I have also ventured to suggest, according to my own observation and experience, that either the Court has not yet secured the proper method of selecting and appointing officials, or that the officials themselves are not permitted to make full and free use of their powers.

These matters I regard as of first importance to your own enlightenment. If I were to hold my tongue on such things, and just present for your consideration one or two matters of trifling importance, asking you to estimate their relative benefit or injury, it would merely muddle your mind and be of no practical help to the government of the country. To act in that way would be foreign to my ideas of loyalty, so I trust your Majesty will give my proposals your careful attention, adopting such as you may think beneficial and appropriate. That I am convinced will make for the increasing well-being of your people.

Current Extravagance

THE people are the special object of Heaven's love and nurturing care, but the ruler is the one on whom they set their hope (for the maintenance of the means of life). The Sages, in accordance with Heaven's ideas, established rulers for the people, with the main object of securing peace and ensuring prosperity for them. These things depend upon the proper regulation of public life and the maintenance of correct customs. Any change that takes place in such matters is of vital consequence to the life of the people, and in proportion as their spirit is affected so the prosperity or decadence of the State is at stake. It is, therefore, a question to which the most careful attention should be given.

The good ruler maintains an economical standard in public life, extravagance being recognized as a great evil. If extravagance is not controlled it soon reaches an irremediable stage, when the people, in order to satisfy their lust for power and prestige, are ready to exhaust all their resources.

It should be remembered that the productive activity of Heaven is limited by the seasons, and that the power of men to avail themselves of such is limited also. But the state expenditure is incessant and knows no bounds. Unless some method of control is devised, then the wealth gathered at these fixed seasons and by this limited means, will lead to the poverty of the people on the one hand and the reckless extravagance (of certain classes) on the other.

Since the inauguration of the Sung Dynasty, thanks to a succession of four sage-like rulers, the empire has gradually been reduced to order, and the laws and constitution have been definitely promulgated. Taxation has not been of an overburdensome character, and public services have been equitably apportioned. The present has never been surpassed for its tranquillity.

In view of these considerations, it should follow as a matter of course that every family should have enough for its needs, and every man sufficient for his maintenance.

Yet the facts are otherwise. The poorer classes cannot clothe their children properly, even in the coarsest of cloth. The serving and laboring classes persist in their cunning and deceitful practices. The reason for this is that we have not eliminated corrupt and pernicious customs.

The influence of the Sage proceeds from that which is near to what is more remote, from within to without. The capital city is the place where the fashions are set, the centre toward which the faces of the people are turned, and the standards of which they are inclined to imitate.

It is difficult to get the official clan, with their wealth and abundance of possessions, to adopt an economical way of life. They readily fall into extravagance. On occasions of ceremony their raiment and equipages

From H. R. Williamson, *Wang An Shih,* London: Arthur Probsthain, 1935, 2 vols., I: 114–117. Reprinted by permission.

are marvellous. They make constant changes in their utensils, and other appurtenances. The influence of all this rapidly spreads throughout the land.

The consequence is that the artisan class devote themselves to the production of useless articles, and the commercial world concentrates on the securing of rare goods which by their very nature are difficult to obtain. The desire for strange and wonderful things grows from year to year, and ability to make frequent changes becomes estimable. So we find that a thing is cast aside before it is damaged at all, and that those who still follow the old fashions are made a laughing stock.

The rich strive to outstrip their fellows, and the poor are ashamed of their poverty. The latter say, "I too am a man. I suffer lack while he (the rich) gets honors and possessions in such abundance." So they turn to ways of envy and emulation, devoting their whole energies to the attempt to outstrip their fellows. The result is that among the lower strata of society there are those who exhaust the resources of a lifetime in one mad moment of extravagance. But there is no forest so big that it cannot be consumed by a prairie fire, and no sea or river so large that it can ever fill a leaking vessel.

When modest and simple customs are cast aside, covetous and corrupt practices become the norm. This in its turn leads to the exhaustion of the resources of both high and low. The people generally become depraved and the officials lose their reputation for honesty. Cruelty and oppression come to be regarded as the proper course while those who are of a dutiful and self-respecting character are considered base and uncultured.

The economically minded and upright become few, while the money-grabbers get numerous. The wealth of the rich parades itself in every corner of the city, while the corpses of the poor fill the ditches in the wild.

It is but natural for a man to take pleasure in life when his mind and body are free from anxiety and distress, and that when his mind is troubled by physical suffering he begins to lose his desire to live.

In such a case as this the laws are powerless to prevent trouble. In fact this is the very reason why the penal code is not respected, or effectively administered.

A great flood may be caused by a small hole in the river bank and a tiny sprout may grow up into an enormous tree. It is easier to prohibit certain things at the beginning than to save the situation later on.

So we ought to take steps akin to the practice of the ancient rulers, and demand that all wares be handed in for inspection before being put on the market. All who are producing articles of a useless, extravagant or immoral character, or anything which is inclined to deprave the people, should be punished. Such articles and utensils as are permitted to be used by various grades of society should be classified with a view to limiting the expenditure on such things.

Artisans and merchants who are promoting the production and sale of luxuries should be heavily taxed to make their trade difficult and shameful. When the people perceive that it is useless to go on producing articles of luxury, and that punishment and shame await those who carry on the trade, they will be forced into the fields, and as more land is brought under cultivation, there will be no lack of food.

If this is made clear to all, the control that is exercised in the capital will naturally lead to the whole country being brought into line.

JUDGMENT OF CONTEMPORARIES

Impeachment of Wang An-shih

LÜ HUI

As a member of the Censorate, the body charged with investigating and reporting to the Emperor on the state of his government, Lü Hui was well within his duties in submitting the following list of charges. However, H. R. Williamson, who translated the selection below, follows the opinion of the Chinese scholar Liang Ch'i-ch'ao that Lü's attack was motivated by personal anger. It would tax our space to try to describe the circumstances referred to in each of his charges, but the attempt to make Wang out to be an immoral man is clear from the list as it stands. The memorial, submitted in 1069, brought no action from the Emperor, and Lü resigned his post in the capital to become a regional official.

1. Wang An Shih proudly refused to make apology for a wrong decision in connection with the case of the fighting quail, although called upon to do so.

He made various pretexts for refusing to accept the calls of the Emperor Ying Tsung to take office under him, but promptly accepted your (i.e. Shen Tsung's) call to the governorship of Chiang Ning Fu, just because it happened to suit his personal convenience. This attitude toward Ying Tsung shows his insolence.

2. Wang An Shih refused to take small appointments but avidly accepted the governorship of Chiang Ning Fu and a place on the Literary Council (Han Lin Yuan). In these matters he was ruled by considerations of personal advantage only, paying no regard to moral principles.

3. Wang An Shih, in his capacity as teacher to the Emperor, appealed that he might sit in the Imperial presence, thus not only demonstrating his ignorance of correct distinctions, but also his tendency to self-glorification.

4. Since Wang An Shih has assumed office as vice-Grand Councillor he has repeatedly remained behind after Imperial audiences for private conversation with the Emperor. He has taken advantage of such opportunities to bring pressure to bear upon the Emperor to affix his seal to certain documents, thus preventing action of an opposing character from his associates. If such matters turned out well he would take credit to himself, if ill, he would lay the blame upon the Emperor.

5. In making decisions on important cases-at-law like that of the Teng Chow Fu assault incident, he was actuated by purely personal motives. He thus made a travesty of public justice.

6. Wang An Shih pressed the claims of his brother An Kuo for official appointment, and exacted vengeance of the examiner who failed to give him high place at the examination. During the six months since he came into high office, he had presumed on his influence to an altogether unwarranted degree. None dared to oppose his will, but

From H. R. Williamson, *Wang An Shih,* London: Arthur Probsthain, 1935, 2 vols., II: 102–107. Reprinted by permission.

those who sought his favor rushed to his door in crowds. His tendency to form private factions was already a great menace to public life.

7. Wang An Shih has made appointments entirely on his own authority, transferring court officers who were not of his own party to outside positions. For these he professed to have the Emperor's authority, but actually issued the orders in his own name. He has thus exceeded the bounds of his legitimate authority, and broken long-established precedent. By his arrogance and assumption in this matter he has transgressed the principles of good government.

8. Wang An Shih is overbearing in his relations with his associates, and brooks no opposition. He was so furious with T'ang Chieh for his opposition that a disgraceful scene was enacted in the Imperial presence. Later on T'ang Chieh succumbed to his chagrin, dying of a carbuncle which broke out on his back as a result of this incident. Wang An Shih had no consideration for anybody but himself and for no other opinion than his own.

9. When the proposal was made that your Majesty's brother Ch'i Wang should be removed from the Court, Wang An Shih opposed you when you demanded that the man who suggested this infamous proposal, Chang Pi Kuang, should be punished. He has thus lent his support to a policy of separating the members of the royal family.

10. Wang An Shih has gradually seized control of all finances of the State and in collaboration with his partisans in the Board of War, is scheming to get all military and financial authority into his own hands. He has appointed three of his own faction to high office, and commissioned eight of them to travel through the country on the pretext of devising measures of financial economy, but really with a view to throwing the whole country into turmoil. The injurious character of his policy is already apparent, and so far no one can see any advantage accruing from it.

Memorial to Emperor Shen-tsung on the New Laws of Wang An-shih

SU SHIH

Su Shih (1037–1101), also known by his pen-name Su Tung-p'o, was one of two famous sons of a famous father, Su Hsün. An outstanding poet, calligrapher, and painter as well as a public official, Su Shih was initially sympathetic to the aims of Wang An-shih, but was subsequently driven from court because of his outspoken opposition to the New Laws. In this eloquent memorial, which suggests something of his famous prose style, Su criticizes especially the new labor service, crop loan, and state marketing systems. Note his complaint that Wang's original proposal concerning the marketing system seemed to have been deliberately vague and seemingly innocuous, as if to hide Wang's real intentions.

WHAT a ruler has to rely upon is only the hearts of men. Men's hearts are to the ruler what roots are to a tree, what oil is to a lamp, water to fish, fields to a farmer, or money to a merchant.

Now Your Majesty knows that the hearts of the people are not happy. Men, whether within the court or outside, whether worthy or unworthy, all say that from the founding of the dynasty to the present, the fiscal administration of the empire has been entrusted solely to the commissioner, assistant commissioners, and the supervisors of the Finance Commission, who for more than one hundred years have left no matter untended. Now, for no cause, another commission has been set up in the name of "Coordinating the Policies of the Three Fiscal Offices." [1] Six or seven young men are made to discuss fiscal policies day and

night within the bureau, while more than forty aides are sent out to explore the situation. The vast scale of their initial operations has made people frightened and suspicious; the strangeness of the new laws adopted has made officials fearful and puzzled. Worthy men seek for an explanation, and failing to get any, cannot relieve their anxiety; small men simply conjecture as to what is going on at court and give voice to slander, saying that Your Majesty, as the master of 100,000 chariots [i.e., of a large empire and army] is interested in personal profit, and the official in charge of the government administration, as the chancellor of the Son of Heaven, is concerned with controlling wealth. Business is at a standstill and the prices of goods have been rising. From places as near as the Huai River region to places as far as Szechwan, hundreds of mouths are talking and hundreds of views are expressed. Some

[1] Or, Finance Planning Commission [Editor's note]

From Wm. Theodore de Bary, Wing-tsit Chan, and Burton Watson, eds., *Sources of Chinese Tradition*, New York: Columbia University Press, 1960, pp. 480–486 (including headnote). Reprinted by permission.

21

say that the main store in the capital [a sarcastic reference to the central government and its business activities] is considering the establishment of superintendencies, that there is going to be a prohibition on [private production of] wine in the mountain wilds of Kweichow, that monks and nuns in permanent residence [at monasteries or nunneries] are to be arrested, and that the salaries of officials and soldiers are to be reduced. Statements like these are countless. And it is even said that the government intends to restore the punishment of mutilation. . . .

Now the Commission to Coordinate Fiscal Administration has the reputation of seeking for profit, while the six or seven young men and their forty or more aides are instruments for the pursuit of profit. . . . The man who plunges into the forest with a pack of hunting dogs and then protests, "I am not hunting," would do better to get rid of the hunting dogs and then the animals will not be so frightened. The man who takes out fishing nets and heads for the water, but then protests, "I am not going fishing," would do better to get rid of the fish nets and then men would believe him. Therefore your servant considers that in order to expunge the slander, to call forth harmonious feelings, to restore public confidence, and put the nation at rest, nothing better could be done than to abolish the Commission to Coordinate Fiscal Policies. The purpose of Your Majesty in establishing this office was but to promote advantages [or profits] and eliminate disadvantages. So if abolishing it does not promote advantages and eliminate disadvantages, then it should not be abolished; but if abolishing it makes all in the empire happy and puts their hearts at peace, then there is certainly nothing wrong with what promotes such advantages while removing disadvantages. Why, then, should it not be abolished? . . .

Since ancient times men drafted from the households in each district have always had to be used for local services. It is just the same as the five grains always having

to be used for food, hemp having to be used for clothing, boats having to be used for crossing rivers, or bullocks and horses having to be used for traveling on land. Although sometimes other things have been used instead, still in the long run this could not be made a regular practice throughout the empire. Now some people have heard that in the region of Chekiang and Kiangsu, a few prefectures hire men to perform these services, and they want to extend this practice throughout the empire. This is like seeing the dates and chestnuts of Peking and Shansi, or the taro root of Szechwan, and then advocating that the five grains be done away with. How could that be made feasible? Besides, they want the proceeds from government factories to be used for the hiring of public storage and transport officers.[2] Although they are expected to render long-term service, they receive meager payment for their labors. Since they receive so little for such long service, from now on they may be expected gradually to fall away and go elsewhere. How seriously this will affect the whole basis and functioning of local governments can well be imagined! . . .

Although in recent years, households in the rural districts have been allowed to hire men [to perform these services], nevertheless, if these hired men ran away, the households still had the responsibility [of replacing them]. Now in addition to the Twice-A-Year Tax, another tax item has been introduced called the labor charge, which pays for the government's hiring of men. Thus the government has taken upon itself the responsibility for the hiring of men. Since Yang Yen in the T'ang dynasty abolished the system of [land] taxes in grain, labor taxes [on able-bodied men], and the cloth exaction [on households], and replaced it with the Twice-A-Year Tax, the sum of all taxes collected in

[2] Ya-chien ["Office Service"]—a type of local service involving responsibility for the storage and transportation of goods or property. Considered extremely burdensome, this responsibility was previously assigned to and rotated among the more well-to-do families, who often tried to evade it,

the fourteenth year of Ta-li [779] was used as the basis for determining the rate of the Twice-A-Year Tax. Thus the land, labor, and cloth taxes were all combined in the Twice-A-Year Tax. Yet now, while the Twice-A-Year Tax is kept as before, how can a labor tax again be demanded? When a sage introduces a law he always takes thousands of generations into consideration. How can we add another item to the regular taxes? . . .

Households of which a female is head and those with only a single male are the most unfortunate of all under Heaven. The first concern of the ancient kings was to show them compassion; and yet now the first concern of Your Majesty is to make them [pay for] local services. These are the households in which the family line will be discontinued when its present members die or those in which the only male is still too young. If several years were allowed the latter, he would become an adult, render service, grow old and die, and have his property confiscated by the government [since there is no one to inherit it]. How can a ruler, so rich as to possess all within the four seas, have the hardness of heart not to take pity on such persons? . . .

There has long been a prohibition against the practice of crop loans. Now Your Majesty has inaugurated the system and made it a regular practice year after year. Although it is declared that there shall be no compulsion to make people take the loans, nevertheless after several generations, if there should be oppressive rulers and corrupt officials, can Your Majesty guarantee that there will be no compulsion? In the days ahead this system will be hated by all under Heaven and it will be recorded in the dynastic history that the crop-loan system began with Your Majesty. What a pity! Besides, when silk was bought in the Southeast, payment was originally supposed to be in cash, while in obtaining horse fodder from Shensi, cash was not allowed in commutation. Edicts were issued by the court and the officials usually enforced them. Nevertheless, salt is always ac-

cepted now in payment for silk and cash is allowed in commutation for fodder. From this we can see that the declaration against the use of compulsion in the taking of crop loans is also an empty formality. . . .

Even if the regulations are strictly enforced and there is really no compulsion, those people and households who would willingly apply for it must be the poor and the families in need, for if they had any surplus of their own, why would they come and do business with the government? But when the [poor] people are whipped and pressed to the extreme, they will run away, and when they have run away, their debts to the government will be apportioned among their neighbors who are collectively responsible. Such a course can have no other outcome; logically it could not be otherwise.

Moreover, of all such measures the ever-normal granary may be considered the best. It is modest in what it seeks to preserve and yet far-reaching in its effects. Suppose a county of 10,000 households has only 1,000 bushels of grain in storage. When the price of grain is high, if the 1,000 bushels are put on the market, the prices of goods are kept stable. When the price of goods in the market is kept stable, there is a sufficiency of food in the land. There is no hoarding of grain by some while others beg for food, no pursuing and pressing by the headman of the village to make people pay back their loans. Now if the ever-normal granary is converted to a crop-loan fund, and one bushel of grain is lent to each household, then what will be done to relieve the hunger of all those besides the 1,000 households [so provided for]? Besides, there is always the fear that the government funds of the ever-normal granary will prove insufficient. If all the funds are used up to buy the grain, then none will be left for money lending; if the fund is held for lending purposes, then very little grain will be bought. Thus we see that the ever-normal granary and the crop-loan system are by nature incompatible. How much can we expect to achieve by it, if we destroy one for the accomplishment of the other? The government will incur a deficit and the people will incur harm. However much we may regret it later, what can be done then? . . .

During the time of Emperor Wu of Han, the financial resources of the nation were exhausted, and the proposal of the merchant, Sang Hung-yang, to buy commodities when prices were cheap and sell them when prices were dear was adopted. This was called Equal Distribution. Thereupon business came to a standstill and banditry became widespread. This almost led to revolution. When Emperor Chao ascended the throne, scholars all rose up in opposition to the theory of [Sang]. Ho Kuang [the chief minister] heeded the desires of the people and granted their request that the system be abandoned. Then all under Heaven were reconciled to the throne and no further trouble arose. It is surprising to hear this kind of proposal raised again. When this law was first introduced, it sounded as if very little was involved. They said merely that goods bought cheaply here should be transferred elsewhere when prices were high, using supplies near at hand to ease scarcity afar. But offices and staffs have been set up all over, and a large amount of cash has been appropriated. The big and wealthy merchants have all become suspicious and dare not move. They believe that although it has not been openly declared that the government will engage in buying and selling, nevertheless, permission has been given to exchange commodities, and it has never been heard that the government engages in the exchange of goods without competing with the merchants for profit. The business of merchants is very complicated and is difficult to practice. When they buy, they give money in advance; when they sell, they collect the money afterward. Many are the means they use to supplement each other; intricate and involved are their dealings. By these means, their twofold profit is obtained. Now for the government to buy such and such a commodity, it must first set up offices and staffs, so that the expense for clerical and fiscal services is considerable at the outset. If not of good quality, an item will not be bought; if not paid for in cash, an item cannot be purchased. Therefore the price paid by the government must be higher than that paid by the people. And when the government sells goods, it will still suffer the disadvantages mentioned before. How can the government get the same profit as the merchant? The court has not taken these factors into consideration, and yet has appropriated 5,000,000 cash for this venture. Once the money is disbursed, I fear it cannot be collected again. Even should there be some slight gain from it, the loss in revenue from taxes on merchants will certainly be greater. . . .

The preservation or loss of a nation depends upon the depth or shallowness of its virtue, not upon its strength or weakness. The length or shortness of a dynasty depends upon the stoutness or flimsiness of its social customs, not upon its richness or poverty. If its moral virtue is truly deep and its social customs are truly stout, even though the country is poor and weak, its poverty and weakness will not affect its duration and existence. If its virtue is shallow and its social customs flimsy, even though the nation is rich and strong, this will not save it from coming to an early end. When a ruler knows this, he knows what is important and what is not important. Therefore the wise rulers of ancient times did not abandon virtue because the country was weak, nor did they permit social customs to suffer because the country was poor. . . .

A Petition to Do Away with the Most Harmful
of the New Laws

SSU-MA KUANG

Ssu-ma Kuang (1019–1086) was one of the giants among the scholar-states-
men of the Confucian revival in the eleventh century. He had already had a
long and distinguished career in high office when he left the government in
1070 out of opposition to Wang An-shih's policies, and devoted himself to
writing his monumental general history of China. Following the death of Wang's
patron, the Emperor Shen-tsung, Ssu-ma Kuang served briefly as prime minister
before his own death, and was responsible for the abolition of many of Wang's
reforms.

YOUR servant sees that the late emperor was sagacious and intelligent,
did his utmost to govern well, and sought
to employ an able man to assist him in
achieving peace and order. This man was
entrusted with the administration of government. His advice was acted upon, and
his plans were followed. Nothing could
ever come between them. . . . [The late
emperor] was indeed an extraordinary
ruler, such as not every generation produces
and even in a thousand years is rarely met
with. Unfortunately the one in whom he
placed his trust was a man who largely
failed to understand the feelings of men
and the principles of things, and who
could not fulfill the expectations of his
sage master. He was self-satisfied and self-
opinionated, considering himself without
equal among the men of the past and
present. He did not know how to select
what was best in the laws and institutions
of the imperial ancestors and to bring together the happiest proposals put forth

throughout the empire, so as to guide the
imperial intelligence and assist in accomplishing the great task. Instead he often
adulterated the traditional regulations with
his own ideas, which he termed "The New
Laws." Whatever this man wanted to do
could neither be held up by the ruler nor
changed by the people. Those who agreed
with him were given his help in rising to
the sky, while those who differed with him
were thrown out and cast down into the
ditch. All he wanted was to satisfy his own
ambitions, without regard to the best interests of the nation.

Human inclinations being what they
are, who does not love wealth and high
rank, and who does not fear punishment
and misfortune? Seeing how the wind
blew and following with the current, the
officials and gentry vied in proposing
schemes, striving to be clever and unusual.
They abandoned what was right and
picked up what was wrong; they supported
what was harmful and rejected what was

From Wm. Theodore de Bary, Wing-tsit Chan, and Burton Watson, eds., Sources of Chinese Tradition, New York: Columbia University Press, 1960, pp. 486–489 (including headnote). Reprinted by
permission.

25

beneficial. In name they loved the people; in fact they injured the people. In name they benefited the nation; in fact they did the nation harm. The crop loans, the local service exemption, the marketing controls, the credit and loan system, and other measures were introduced. They aimed at the accumulation of wealth and pressed the people mercilessly. The distress they caused still makes for difficulties today. Besides, there were frontier officers who played fast and loose hoping to exploit their luck. They spoke big and uttered barefaced lies, waged war unjustifiably and needlessly disturbed the barbarians on our borders. . . . They strewed the wastelands with the skeletons of so many hundreds of thousands of soldiers and abandoned hundreds of millions in weapons and goods in strange lands. Besides, officials who liked to create new schemes which they might take advantage of to advance themselves suggested setting up the collective security militia system (*pao-chia*), horse-raising system, and the horse-care system,[1] as a means of providing for the military establishment. They changed the regulations governing the tea, salt, iron, and other monopolies, and increased the taxes on family property, on [buildings] encroaching on the street,[2] on business, and so forth, in order to meet military expenses. The result was to cause the people of the nine provinces to lose their livelihood and suffer extreme distress, as if they had been cast into hot water and fire. All this happened because the great body of officials were so eager to advance themselves. They misled the late emperor, and saw to it that they themselves derived all the profit from these schemes while the emperor incurred all the resent-

ment. This was not at all what the late emperor had originally intended. . . .

Now the evils of the New Laws are known to everyone in the empire, high or low, wise or ignorant. Thus when Your Majesty revised these laws to even a slight extent, all the people near and far congratulated each other. Yet there are still some measures which are harmful to the people and hurtful to the state, which have many disadvantages and no advantages, such as the collective security militia system, the local service exemption payment, and the general commanderies. These three matters are of immediate and urgent importance, and are the first of the things which should be abolished. Your servant is going to report on them in separate memorials, hoping that it may please your sage will to grant us an early decision and act upon them.

Ssu-ma Kuang presented three separate memorials requesting abolition of each of these measures and summarized his reasons in still another memorial as follows:

Your servant has already pointed out that training and inspection of the militia involves a great expenditure of labor and money for both the government and the people, and yet the militia is of no real use in war. To pay money in lieu of local services is easy on the rich and hard on the poor, who must contribute to the support of idlers and vagrants [paid to perform these services]. It results in the peasantry losing their property and being reduced to utter misery, without recourse or appeal. The general commanderies now have absolute control over the army administration, while local civil officials have no authority whatever and no means of coping with emergencies. . . .

The best plan now is to select and keep those new laws which are of advantage to the people and of benefit to the state, while abolishing all those which are harmful to the people and hurtful to the state. This will let the people of the land know unmistakably that the court loves them with

---

[1] These systems were designed to provide horses for the army after the old grazing lands had been occupied by hostile tribes. Under the horse-raising system (*hu-ma*) people bought horses which, when raised, were sold to the government. Under the horse-care system (*pao-ma*) the government provided the horses or the funds to buy them and the people were expected to take care of them for the militia. In either case horses that died had to be replaced at the individual's expense.

[2] A tax on roadside stalls, kiosks, etc.

a paternal affection. Those officials who are oppressive will be bound to change and serve loyally. Those people who have been estranged and embittered are bound to change and give their support and approbation to the court. This worthy achievement will be crowned with glory, and there will be no end to the blessings it bestows. Would this not be splendid?

LATER JUDGMENTS

Memorial to Wang An-shih

LU HSIANG-SHAN

Lu Hsiang-shan, or Lu Chiu-yüan (1139–1192), is most famous as a proponent of the school of thought known in the Confucian revival as the school of the Mind, or Intuition. In this a philosophical opponent of Chu Hsi, the next man represented in these selections and the principal figure of the school of Principle, or Law, Lu nevertheless assessed Wang An-shih in terms with which Chu Hsi could agree.

WANG AN SHIH, working in collaboration with the Emperor Shen Tsung, sincerely endeavoured to revive the illustrious age of Yao and Shun. The confidence which Shen Tsung reposed in his minister was of such a character that, in the words of Tseng Lu Kung, "Wang An Shih should have been willing to sacrifice life itself in order to justify it." It is evident from succeeding history that Wang An Shih lived up to his own advice to the emperor, viz., "that both ruler and minister should work to the limits of their capacity and strength in the fulfilment of their duty to the people, regardless of consequences or reward."

It is, however, most unfortunate that Wang An Shih failed to fulfil the great purpose of his life, his knowledge being inadequate to the carrying out of his noble intention.

During the reign of the Emperor Jen Tsung, Wang An Shih was called to Court to report on his work in Chiang Tung. He then submitted his memorial of ten thousand words which was a just and candid exposition of current affairs. In this he analysed in detail the defective character of the government. It was a most timely and apposite document.

This memorial was the basis for Wang An Shih's various proposals for reform, and to the practical execution of which he devoted his energies during the first half of Shen Tsung's reign. The main thesis of this memorial was that current methods of government were not in line with the ancient pattern. It was this consummate passion of his (for the restoration of the ancient regime) which contributed in large measure to his failure to carry out the great purpose of his life. For the imitation of Yao and Shun need not necessarily imply that their various measures should be revived in every detail.

However, those critics who described him as a fawning courtier, or an opportunist, or as one who had relinquished his former principles, or as one who violated his principles by plausible but erroneous arguments, with the object of gaining prestige and influence, cannot be said to know Wang An Shih.

When men find themselves at loggerheads with one another, they invariably indulge in slanderous vilification. Men like Chang An Tao, Lü Hsien K'o, and Su Ming Yun,[1] who attacked his character

[1] These are different designations for Chang Fang P'ing, Lü Hui, and Su Hsün.

From H. R. Williamson, *Wang An Shih*, London: Arthur Probsthain, 1935, 2 vols., II: 114–118. Reprinted by permission.

prior to his assuming high office, were of this type. Wang An Shih had his defects, but they were not of the kind which these attributed to him.

For he was a man of heroic mould and will, entirely free from love of luxury, vice, wealth, or even fame. He stood aloof from those who pursued a merely conventional policy in such matters. He was an outstanding example of moral purity and determination. And as for his ideal, his purpose was to sweep the country clean of merely conventional practices, and to eliminate every trace of the *laissez-faire* policy of those officials who either refused to recognize, or failed to see, the necessity for administrative reforms. He sought to follow Confucius and Mencius in matters of principle, and to equal the achievements of I Yin and Chow Kung in affairs of government. He himself was free from all desire for fame, and yet at one time his reputation was so great that some of the most famous men of his day were ready to act as his subordinates. Can this be said to have been accidental?

He was fortunate in having gained the ear and confidence of Shen Tsung, one of the great sovereigns of history, who, after having sat at his feet, called him to be high minister of state. In this, Shen Tsung shows himself a worthy successor of Ch'eng T'ang in his appointment of I Yin and of Kao Tsung in his appointment of Fu Yueh. Whenever Wang An Shih suspected the slightest wavering of Shen Tsung's confidence, he resigned on the pretext of ill-health, and only when the Emperor had given him satisfactory proofs of regret and complete confidence, would he return to his post.

When the new laws were being drawn up and promulgated, discussion became rife and the whole Court resounded with turbulent criticism. Before they had been long in actual operation, opposition was roused from every quarter. Wang An Shih then sought to buttress up his position by reinterpreting the Chow Li, giving lucid and detailed interpretations from this (as being

in line with his proposals), and was so confident that his ideas were right that he pressed them with increased determination and resolution.

This led to strenuous opposition on the part of the high officials of the time, and one by one they left the Court. Meaner men seized their opportunity. They cleverly availed themselves of the opening which his determination presented for flattery, with the result that the loyal and honest deserted him, and the crafty got their way. Wang An Shih failed to perceive the peril of all this, and this must be accounted a defect.

One would hesitate to say that each of the measures propounded by Wang An Shih was absolutely perfect or that he adopted the right way of reforming the abuses of his times. His opponents were not sufficiently conscientious and he was excessively determined. So that both sides failed to make the contribution for which the times called.

But this consideration may be urged in his favour. Those who attacked his policy in the main excessively slandered him, but failed to produce adequate reasons for their detractions. Very few indeed took up what may be termed a moderate attitude, the vast majority adopting an extreme position. So they not only failed to gain the support of the Emperor for their views, but failed also to convince Wang An Shih of the error of his ways. On the contrary, their opposition, being of the type it was, only served to increase his determination to carry out his ideas. So his opponents must share the blame for whatever guilt attaches to the promoters of the reforms.

The great officials of the earlier part of Che Tsung's reign, in their rescindment of his measures, were not free from prejudices of a partisan character. The worth of the jewel lies in the fact that its flaws as well as its fine points are both clearly revealed. That the ancient records are reliable is due to the fact that affairs were honestly recorded, regardless of their being right or wrong, good or bad. As the records are free from partiality, they serve for the encouragement or warning of succeeding generations.

But when facts are concealed, or unduly emphasized, when facts are only partially recorded or spurious additions are made to them, with the idea of making the records conform to one's personal likes and dislikes, violence is done to one's conception of real scholarship. For mean folk are thereby afforded an excellent pretext for exacting vengeance on their opponents.

Wang An Shih roused the ire of his political opponents by terming them mere conventionalists, or mean fellows. When his opponents were restored to power they altered everything which he had introduced. Chagrin played its part in this, and no one can deny that they went beyond what the circumstances called for. Later again in the times of Shao Sheng (1094-8), when the pendulum swung again in Wang An Shih's favour, the actions taken against his political opponents were due to the extreme and unwarranted attitude of their predecessors, so the blame for this is not all to be laid at Wang An Shih's door. From that time on to the period Ts'ung Ning (1102-7) the political pendulum swung to and fro. The spirit of faction and feud wrought dire results. But chief blame attaches to the historiographers of the times of Yuan Yu, i.e. 1086-1094, for the way in which they recorded the events of Hsi Ning's time, i.e. 1068-1078. For this incited unworthy men to adopt the revival of Wang An Shih's policy as a pretext for exacting vengeance on their political opponents. Both sides suffered from this.

Modern scholars, who fill the schools with their prejudiced opinions about Wang An Shih, cannot be termed good students of history (i.e. they are unable to distinguish between right and wrong in the attitudes of their predecessors).

The neglect in which Wang An Shih and the work which he accomplished have been allowed to lie, is due to this prevalence of unfavorable criticism and fear of taking his side. All the more commendable, therefore, is this act of the magistrate Ch'ien in undertaking the restoration of this memorial shrine. The shrines of goblins and sprites are nowadays maintained in the best repair, but if Mr. Ch'ien had not taken the matter in hand, the shrine of Wang An Shih, the hero of his day, who resisted the evil tendencies of his time with a character of outstanding worth, and with ability such as is unequalled by the spirits of hills and streams, would have remained in a grievously dilapidated condition.

I take it that you, Wang An Shih, although you refused to heed the opinions of your contemporaries, will not be altogether displeased with what I have written about you in this tablet.

Wang An-shih in Retrospect

CHU HSI

Though Wang's New Laws were largely abolished by Ssu-ma Kuang, after the latter's demise, political forces representing Wang's point of view recouped their strength and held power much of the time until the ignominious fall of the Northern Sung dynasty (1126). Many of Wang's policies were briefly revived and some of them—like his public services system, the local security and militia system, and the type of examination essay he introduced into the civil service system—reappeared in later dynasties. Nevertheless, Wang's reputation among later generations of Confucian scholars was generally low, the majority sympathizing with Ssu-ma Kuang, Su Shih, the Ch'eng brothers, and others who had condemned Wang for his flagrant disregard of "human feelings" (which should not necessarily be interpreted to mean "public opinion") and especially for his suppression of criticism at court. Chu Hsi, the preeminent philosopher of the Sung school whose views became enshrined as orthodox Neo-Confucianism in later dynasties, was a follower of the Ch'eng brothers. In these excerpts from his recorded conversations, however, he attempts a balanced judgment of Wang An-shih's strengths and weaknesses, trying to rise above the partisan passions stirred up in the great era of reform.

WE WERE discussing Wang An-shih's meeting with Emperor Shen-tsung. "It was a chance that comes only once in a thousand years," I said. "Unfortunately Wang's ideas and methods were not correct so that in the end everything went to pieces the way it did." Someone asked: "When Wang An-shih started, was he so self-assured about his methods and tactics, or did he become so only later?" I replied: "At first he felt only that something should be done. But later when other people began to attack him, he became obstinate and unyielding. Unless one reads his diary one has no way of understanding the full story. As a matter of fact he became so overbearing in argument and so contemptuous of everyone around him that men like Wen Lu-kung [Wen Yen-po] did not dare to utter a word." Someone asked about Ssu-ma Kuang's actions. I replied: "He saw only that Wang An-shih was wrong, and this led him to go too far in the other direction. When the whole matter first came under discussion, men like Su Tung-p'o also felt that reforms should be undertaken, but later they all changed their minds completely.". . .

The implementation of the reforms was actually planned by all the statesmen together. Even Ch'eng Hao did not consider them to be wrong, for he felt that the time was ripe for a change. Only later, when everyone's feelings had been aroused, did Ch'eng Hao begin to urge Wang An-shih not to do things that went against human

From Wm. Theodore de Bary, Wing-tsit Chan, and Burton Watson, eds., *Sources of Chinese Tradition,* New York: Columbia University Press, 1960, pp. 489–491 (including headnote). Reprinted by permission.

feelings. Finally, when Wang had rejected the advice of everyone else and was using all his power to enforce his policies, the other statesmen began to withdraw. Tao-fu asked: "If even the man in the street could tell that the implementation of these reforms would be harmful, why was it that Ch'eng Hao did not consider them wrong?" I replied: "The harm came from the way that Wang put them into practice. If Ch'eng Hao had been doing it, things would certainly not have ended up in the mess they did." It was asked: "What would have been the situation if only [the elder statesmen] Han Ch'i and Fu Pi had been employed in the government?" I replied: "Those two gentlemen would have made no changes at all." "Suppose Ssu-ma Kuang had been in sole charge?" it was asked. "He is altogether a different sort of person again," I said. "If the two Ch'eng brothers had assumed the responsibility," it was asked, "would things not have been different?" I replied: "In the case of Ch'eng Hao things would have been different

provided he had full discretion in all matters.". . .

Jen-chieh remarked that the *pao-chia* [militia] system which Wang An-shih put into effect in the capital area naturally aroused opposition at the start. But when the gentlemen of the Yüan-yu party abolished it entirely, what they did was to upset completely a system that was already well established. "That is quite true," I replied. . . .

It was the opinion of the various worthy men of the Yüan-yu party that in general everything should go according to established ways. Their idea was to correct the mistakes arising from the changes [made by Wang An-shih] during the Hsi-ning and Yüan-feng periods, but they did not realize that they were lapsing into mere stand-pattism. Since the empire exists, soldiers must be trained, abuses must be corrected, and government affairs must be properly ordered. How could one simply do nothing at all? . . .

MODERN REAPPRAISALS

Wang An-shih

JOHN C. FERGUSON

In the article below, John C. Ferguson (1866–1945) conveys the enthusiasm for Wang An-shih that marked the modern "rediscovery" of the New Laws, with their ring of utilitarianism, humanitarianism and progress. The basis of his admiration of Wang seems to be a rather liberal and moral socialism. In finding apparent compatibility between Wang's work and modern political attitudes, Ferguson is representative of much of the twentieth-century approach to the eleventh-century reformer.

WANG AN-SHIH was a product of the age in which he lived. It was the flourishing period of the Sung (Northern Sung) dynasty, during which military glory was added to the more permanent blessings of peaceful progress. The dynasty was founded by the warrior Chao, who had led his troops successfully against various rivals and Tartar enemies. Though he was not above the vices of camp-life, yet after his proclamation as Emperor by his military commanders, he gave himself to the establishment of peace and to the restoration of prosperity to the people. During the reigns of his two successors, the power of the dynasty was extended over several feudal kings to the west and south, and the Empire was divided into fifteen provinces. . . . The capital was well separated from the Khitans and other Tartar tribes, but war was carried against them into their own borders, and under the Emperor Chen-Tsung the Khitans suffered a severe defeat, the good effects of which, however, were weakened by the subsequent treaty in which the Emperor promised to make yearly payments of silver and silk. A regency of ten years under the Empress Dowager Liu greatly disturbed the general prosperity and incited the Khitans to send an ambassador to Jen Tsung demanding the cession of territory, but by the skilful diplomacy of the Minister Fu Pi, these demands were changed into an increase of yearly gifts. However, the humiliating addition was made in the new treaty that these yearly gifts were to be considered as tribute. Fan Chung-yen also secured a victory over Yuan, the ruler of Hsia, who promised to acknowledge the Emperor as his Lord. The result of these two treaties of peace was to give the Emperor Jen-tsung a feeling of security and to enable him to solidify the government of his country. He surrounded himself with men of great ability—scholars, statesmen and patriots—and these men continued their influence through the reign of his successor Ying-tsung and into the reign of Shen-tsung. In addition to Fu Pi and Fan Chung-yen, already mentioned, there were Ssu-ma Kuang, Ou-yang Hsiu, Han Ch'i, Lü Hui-Ch'ing and Wang An-shih.

The period of time in which Wang An-shih came into prominence is, roughly speaking, A.D. 1055 to 1085. It was the

From *Journal of the Royal Asiatic Society, North China Branch* 35:65–75 (1903–4). [The romanization of some Chinese words has been changed to the more conventional Wade-Giles system.]

35

time in Europe when the struggle between the Empire and the Papacy was approaching a climax, during which the great Hildebrand came into power and did so much to shape the future policy of the Papacy. Both East and West were in a turmoil in which great minds could assert themselves. A contrast between Europe and China at this period would show that China was in a more peaceful and more prosperous condition than Europe. For this reason it was possible that the socialistic and reformatory schemes of Wang An-shih could be attempted.

One leading characteristic of the Emperors of the Sung dynasty must be noted. They were ever ready to listen to the advice of their ministers and encouraged them to speak frankly. On one occasion Ssu-ma Kuang pointed out to the Emperor Jen-tsung that the benevolent duty of a sovereign to his people was to provide for their education, their maintenance and their prosperity, and that an intelligent sovereign would make it his constant duty to distinguish between good and bad advisers. His advice is known as "The Three Instructions." On another occasion, the Emperor Jen-tsung was complaining to his minister, Han Ch'i, of the scant courtesy shown him by the Empress Dowager. Han Ch'i replied to the Emperor that if he only showed filial respect to the Dowager because she was kind to him, it would be nothing to his credit; but that, if in spite of her ill-treatment, he was filial, it would be a true mark of the sincerity of his heart. This willingness of the Sung Emperors to receive advice even when it was distasteful was another favoring condition for the governmental experiments of Wang An-shih. The open-mindedness of the sovereigns gave a great stimulus to the healthy development of the powerful minds among the ministers of state, and was one of the chief causes which enabled the Sung to add more names to the roll of China's illustrious statesmen and scholars than any other dynasty. . . .

At first Wang An-shih made much of the example of the sages Yao and Shun and of Chow Kung; but later, when he passed from the academic discussion of governmental problems with learned friends to the more difficult task of government administration as Prime Minister, he rather emphasized the present needs of his country, and tried to show that the principles which underlay these needs were the same as those which had helped the early sages to settle the questions of their generation. In following the principles of righteous government there should be unison with the highest ideals of the past; but in method there should be freedom to follow such as were adapted to present needs. This seems to have been the position assumed by Wang An-shih as the basis for his reformatory proposals. In carrying out this principle he laid emphasis upon improving the condition of the people, so that their wealth might increase and their lives become less irksome. In other words, he brought into prominence the material and practical elements of social life rather than the intellectual and moral. One is reminded of the general position taken by Professor Huxley in his "Social Diseases and Worse Remedies" when he says: "What profits it to the human Prometheus that he has stolen the fire of heaven to be his servant and that the spirits of the earth and the air obey him, if the vulture of pauperism is eternally to tear his very vitals and keep him on the brink of destruction?" Professor Huxley maintains the same general position as Wang An-shih in making the material prosperity of the people a question of primary importance. The reforms introduced by Wang, which are now to be treated in detail, rest upon this general principle as their basis.

These reform schemes embraced the (1) State Monopoly of Commerce, (2) Equality of Taxation, (3) Militia Organization and (4) Impressed or Conscripted Labor for the State.[1] In order to carry out his

[1] In our terms, (1) Tribute Transport and Distribution System, (2) Land Survey and Equitable Tax, (3) *Pao-chia* System, (4) Hired-Services System. [Editor's note]

various plans, Wang asked the Emperor Shen-tsung to appoint a Special Council of Three,[2] whose duty would be to inaugurate, develop and administer them. This Council was independent of the ordinary administration of the Boards and was similar in organization to the present Board of State Affairs, Chen-Wu-Chu, which deals with all memorials recommending changes. The Emperor trusted Wang and this Council very fully and gave them a free hand to carry out their ideas.

1. The State Monopoly of Commerce . . . was the most far-reaching in its purpose and the one most bitterly opposed of all the reforms. . . . The produce of a district was to be used first for the payment of taxes, then for the direct use of the district, and the residue was to be purchased by the Government at a cheap price. The Government should then either hold this produce in possession till there was a demand for it in the district at an increased price or should transport it to some other district in need of it. The Government was to undertake, in short, the purchase, transport and sale of all products which were in excess of the local needs of any district. Special officers were appointed to act with the local magistrates in the administration of this huge scheme. It was intended by Wang to provide a fixed market for all products, thus increasing the wealth of the people, and at the same time to give the Government a large revenue from the profits of handling, thus avoiding the necessity of increased taxation. Another feature of the plan was called . . . Verdant Sprouts, or what McGowan calls "State Advances to the Cultivators of the Soil,"[3] by which the Government was to lend to all farmers, at the commencement of sowing time in spring, a fixed sum of money which was to be repaid in the autumn when the crops were gathered. It was probably meant at first to make loans to the needy, but it was finally decided to make loans compulsory, making no distinction between those who

needed the money in order to plant their crops and those who did not. All must alike take the Government's loan and pay interest at the rate of two per cent per mensem. . . .

That such a far-reaching scheme, which penetrated into every enterprise of the people, should be met with intense opposition was only to be expected. Han Ch'i objected that the better class of people would not want to be pauperized by accepting loans from the Government, and that while the poorer class would be ready to take the money in the spring they would be very slow to pay anything back in the autumn. The only method of collection would be to make an assessment upon the district. He called Wang the "Money-making Statesman." Ssu-ma Kuang objected that the scheme would make the rich poor and the poor poorer. Su Ch'e said that even well-intentioned people who drew money in such an easy way in the spring would probably squander it in useless expenditures and would have nothing to repay in the autumn. Fu Pi said that the plan contemplated the collection of wealth by the Government, whereas the proper function was to assist in the diffusion of wealth among the people. The opinion of this scheme of Wang's now held by the literary class is that of Chu Hsi, who said that Wang had only the one idea of making profits for the Government, and that his plan made people weary of their lives while it afforded rascals coveted opportunities for robbing industrious, well-labored citizens. A time of great drought came on and there were many complaints from the people and from officials that the drought showed Heaven's displeasure of the scheme, but Wang stoutly maintained that times of drought and rain were beyond the reach of human power and that they were not affected by his methods of administration. This was indeed a bold stand for even such a strong man as Wang to take. . . .

2. Equality of Taxation— . . . by means of an arbitrary division of the country into squares . . . was another part of Wang's

[2] Finance Planning Commission. [Editor's note]
[3] Farming Loans. [Editor's note]

reform movement. It was found that there had been great inequality in the collection of taxes because of the difficulty of fixing proper boundaries. Taxes were being paid on much less ground than was being actually cultivated. To obviate this abuse, Wang proposed to divide the country into squares of 1,000 *pu* (say 5,000 ft.) on each side. Every year in the ninth moon taxes were to be appraised on each square according to the general average of the producing power of the soil, which was divided into five classes, according to its fertility. . . . The principle of payment according to the fertility of the soil seems quite in harmony with Adam Smith's language in describing what he considered to be equality of taxation. He says: "The subjects of every State ought to contribute to the support of the Government as nearly as possible in proportion to their respective abilities; that is, in proportion to the revenue which they respectively enjoy under the protection of the State." The great difference in Wang's scheme was that it was an amount fixed upon the fertility of a district independent of the number of inhabitants. The scheme seems to have been complicated and to have covered more than was necessary to secure the purposes for which it was inaugurated. It would seem that a simple re-survey of the land of each owner would have been sufficient and would not have involved any controversy with individual owners. As it was, Wang's division into squares broke down from the difficulty of excluding from a given square any parts of it such as hills or sand-banks which were not arable. The whole plan was abandoned soon after the death of Shen-tsung, and it cannot be said ever to have come into effective operation.

3. Militia Organization—Pao-chia—is a name with which we are still familiar in Chinese local administration. Wang's plan was to organise every ten families into one section—Pao—over which a headman— Paochang—should be placed; fifty families were to be a large section over which a higher headman should have the jurisdic-

tion, and ten of these large sections should form a district. In every home which had more than one son, one must serve as a militiaman. These men were to be provided with bows and were to be regularly drilled. Each large section was to provide for five men to act as night patrol. Apprehenders of criminals were to be rewarded and any district which concealed criminals was to be fined. The whole of the police and defence of the country was to be in charge of the militia, and each section was to be held responsible for the discipline of its men and for its good order. . . .

In various forms the system has been revived by the Emperors of the Ming and Ch'ing dynasties. Ch'eng-hua and Hung-chih, at the latter part of the fifteenth century, introduced the military side, and Ch'ien-lung, in the middle of the eighteenth century, introduced the police side under an elaborate system which has remained to the present time. The Boxer movement three years ago was founded upon the idea of a defensive militia, and its organization used many of the terms which have been handed down from the time of Wang An-shih. This feature of his reform schemes has had more permanency than any other, and is to be praised for its low estimate of militarism.

4. The last of the great schemes to be noted is that of Impressed or Conscripted Labor for the State. Wang's plan was to do away with the abuses which had grown up around the system of the State's requiring service from its subjects. He proposed to divide the people, including women and the unmarried, into five classes, according to their wealth, and then to issue money to them called . . . help for service, on which interest must be paid at the rate of two per cent per mensem. This interest was to be taken by the State in lieu of labour, which had been formerly required.[4] . . .

These were great schemes for social and political reform introduced by Wang An-

[4] This description is mistaken, for the measure involved taxing the people, not issuing money to them. [Editor's note]

shih. There are many features of his life which I have been obliged to pass over, such as his intimate relations with Lü Hui-ch'ing, his degradation to the Prefecture of Nanking and his death in that city. Neither has it been possible to elaborate upon his relation to the development of the Sung philosophical system. I have endeavoured to confine myself to his reform schemes. The conception of such schemes shows that Wang An-shih was a man of deep thought and broad sympathies. He was of the utilitarian school but his heart was with the suffering populace. His moral enthusiasm never failed him in the face of hostile criticism, and he labored steadily for the good of the people. No suspicion of sordid means or covetous purposes was ever hinted of him. His failing was in being too sanguine of the readiness of the people to fall in with what he considered to be for their good. Though he was practical, he still

sought to conserve the good of the past which had been handed down but was anxious to develop and to improve upon it. The terminology which he invented for reform and reform schemes has been used by all subsequent reformers even down to the Reform Party of our own day. Mr. Lecky, in his "Political Value of History," has observed that "the foundation of the prosperity of nations is laid in pure domestic life, in commercial integrity, in a high standard of moral worth and of public spirit, in simple habits, in courage, uprightness and a certain soundness and moderation of judgment which springs quite as much from character as from intellect." While Wang An-shih laid great stress upon the foundations of prosperity being in the increased wealth of the nation, yet his intense sympathy with the people and his anxiety for their welfare ennobled all his plans with a high standard of moral worth.

Wang An-shih's Reform Policy

H. R. WILLIAMSON

Henry Raymond Williamson's connection with China began in the first decade of the twentieth century, when he went there as a Baptist missionary. His two-volume study of Wang An-shih, from which the selection below has been taken, was submitted as a doctoral dissertation to the University of London. Williamson's admiration of Wang An-shih depends even more clearly than that of John C. Ferguson, the previous writer, on Wang's purpose, as he sees it, of aiding the poor and restricting the rich, the proper instrument for which is the state, working as a regulating and sometimes controlling agency.

I N THE chapter on Wang An Shih's character, we reached the conclusion that the slanderous statements which have found their place in the traditional records cannot be substantiated, and that all the evidence is in favour of his having been a man of pure life and sincere purpose. His literary ability is generally acknowledged to be of a very high order. As an official in the provinces and in minor posts at the capital, he earned a great reputation for devotion to duty, and for administrative ability of exceptional character. But after his assumption of high office under Shen Tsung the policy he inaugurated in collaboration with him, but with which his own name will be for ever associated, met with severe criticism and opposition, and for various reasons all the more famous and influential officials at the Court were compelled to resign their appointments at the capital. But in spite of that fact, until the time of Shen Tsung's death in 1085, Wang An Shih's policy was maintained with little or no change for a period of sixteen or seventeen years.

It is our purpose in this chapter to estimate the character of his political policy. We shall endeavour to evaluate it in essence and results, try to account for the opposition which was aroused and which continued with such persistence, attempt to explain the reason for its abrogation, and assess the popular judgment upon it as represented by Chu Hsi[1] and others. . . .

Briefly, then, the features of his time are as follows, viz.: Foreign aggression in the north and north-west, accompanied by the military weakness and economic stringency of the Sungs. A strong tendency to conservatism and the pursuance of a policy of *laissez-faire* on the part of the great majority of the official clan. A dearth of capable and honest administrators, and the lack of an efficient system whereby this defect could be remedied. A low scale of salaries for those engaged in the various government services conducing to the prevalence of peculation and graft in official circles. A

[1] Chu Hsi, 1130–1200. The major Confucian philosopher of the Sung period and a major scholar in several fields. [Editor's note]

From H. R. Williamson, *Wang An Shih*, London: Arthur Probsthain, 1935, 2 vols., II: 158–182, 184–190, 199–213. Reprinted by permission. [Some of the secondary officials mentioned in this selection are more important for their views in the discussion than for their positions and have not been identified in footnotes.]

tendency amongst the Court officers to form factions. The existence of a powerful capitalistic class upon whom the poorer farmers and traders were dependent for the maintenance of their livelihood, and from whose manipulations of finance the government treasury was losing large sums of possible revenue. These are some of the more prominent characteristics of the age in which Wang An Shih lived.

It is also of first importance to consider the character and purpose of the Emperor Shen Tsung, for they have vital connection with Wang An Shih's policy.

The Dynastic History of Sung, which, as has frequently been pointed out, reflects in the main the opinions of Wang An Shih's political enemies, gives the following résumé of Shen Tsung's character, viz.:

"He sought for public criticism, investigated the conditions under which the people lived, was merciful to the poor and aged, and generous to the distressed."

The nature of the Dynastic Histories being such as has been described above, and containing as they do many signs of dissatisfaction with Shen Tsung for associating himself so closely with Wang An Shih and his policy, it is only natural to infer from the above description, as Liang Ch'i Ch'ao[2] does, that Shen Tsung must have been a really great ruler, one of the greatest since the Ch'in and Han Dynasties. Otherwise the traditional histories could not ascribe to him such characteristics, nor is it likely that he would have been granted the title of "Shen" or "August" as his historical designation.

His purpose was revealed soon after he had ascended the throne, for then it is related that he remarked to Wen Yen Po, "In view of the situation on the frontiers a full treasury is essential for military exigencies." His ancestor in the imperial line, Sung T'ai Tsu, had hoped to inflict a crushing defeat upon the northern bar-

barians, and with that object in view had created a special bank, styled the "Ching Fu Tien," in which he had planned to assemble a sum equal to two million bales of raw silk for military expenses. Shen Tsung soon after his accession changed the name of this bank, and composed the following poem in honour of the occasion:

The five dynasties in succession decayed,
While the northern hordes exceedingly prospered,
I Tsu established the Imperial line,
And formed his plans for revenge.
This special bank he forthwith set up,
With intent to collect a great army,
Can I, his successor, ever forget,
His great and noble purpose?

Later on, Shen Tsung ordered the establishment of thirty-two special banks, in which he intended to accumulate large sums from the revenue surplus. On this occasion he wrote the following lines in commemoration, viz.:

Far into the night I wrack my brain,
Proud of the sacred task,
Committed unto me,
Anxious too,
For I am doubtful of our prowess in arms.
When, oh when, will victory be ours?

Wang Ch'uan Shan[3] says, "Shen Tsung had thoughts to which he dare not give public utterance. The great officers round the throne failed to appreciate his real intent, and so failed to give him the counsel for which he was seeking."

It is evident from this that Shen Tsung's plans were beyond the understanding of his immediate advisers, or at least, beyond their will or capacity to execute. "No wonder," says Liang Ch'i Ch'ao, "when Shen Tsung made the acquaintance of Wang An Shih, and discovered the type of man he was, that he regarded him as his own right hand."

Wang An Shih had the very ideas which he deemed necessary for the carrying out of his great purpose of redeeming the na-

---

[2] Liang Ch'i-ch'ao (1873–1929), one of the leading intellectual figures of his time, was a pioneer in the modern reappraisal of Wang An-shih. His views are strongly reflected in Williamson's work. [Editor's note]

[3] Wang Ch'uan-shan, 1619–1692. Scholar and prolific writer in the period of establishment of Manchu power over China. [Editor's note]

tional shame of many generations, and possessed moreover the right character for putting them into effect. It was but natural, in such circumstances, that the ruler should elect such a man to be his high minister of State, and extend to him his unreserved confidence and wholehearted trust.

Shen Tsung then had as his great purpose the strengthening of the military resources of the empire with a view to thwarting the aggressive tactics of his neighbours in the north and north-west, and even of reclaiming territory which once had been under the sway of the empire in the glorious days of the T'ang Dynasty. It was essential as a corollary to this that the finances of the national treasury should also be greatly increased.

Wang An Shih entered with full sympathy into the plans of the Emperor, and as his high minister of State it was but natural that he should give prime attention to financial and military matters. Chu Hsi makes this a point of severe criticism. In so doing he evidently had in mind the traditional conception of the duties of a high minister of State, in accordance with which such an officer should seek to influence the Emperor by the exposition of moral principles and the rectification of his conduct so that he would, as a matter of course, institute laws which would be both just and beneficent, and make his country prosperous. In line with this traditional conception it would be beneath the dignity of a high minister of State to meddle in such mundane matters as finance and military expeditions.

It is reported that Wang An Shih, shortly after his appointment to high office, suggested to Shen Tsung the possibility of his becoming another Yao and Shun. It was not then foreign to Wang An Shih's ideas that he should use moral suasion or emphasize ethical principles in his relationship with the Emperor, and in the formulation of his policy. His various memorials to the throne are sufficient evidence of that. But at the same time, he perceived that the state of the country demanded practical reforms.

So while not neglecting the importance of ethical considerations, he devoted himself to the creation of a number of political measures tending toward the material prosperity of the empire. "In each and every case," says Liang Ch'i Ch'ao, "his idea was to enhance the prosperity of the state and to improve the people's economic condition."

Ssu Ma Kuang[4] criticized Wang An Shih as being of "unpractical mind," and as "being unacquainted with practical affairs." But the most cursory glance at the character of the various reform measures which he promoted is sufficient to disprove such assertions. He may not have given sufficient consideration to the fact that there were not enough high-minded men in the government service to ensure the success of his different projects, or he may have overlooked the fact that as his measures in the main were directed against the wealthy and influential classes, they would raise such opposition that his measures must eventually fail to produce those permanent results which he expected. Or again he may not have given sufficient thought to the fact that some of his measures would interfere with the customary and easy-going ways of the common people, and that this would make many of his regulations irksome to them. If that is what Ssu Ma Kuang meant by his "being unpractical" or "unacquainted with practical affairs" he may perhaps be considered justified in making the statement. But if he meant that Wang An Shih was ignorant of the need of his country, and lacked the ideas for meeting that need in practical fashion, his criticism is quite beside the mark. Chu Hsi remarks that "the times called for reform and that Wang An Shih had the right ideas for his day."

It is characteristic of Wang An Shih that he combined moral enthusiasm with a "penchant" for practical politics, as we trust will appear in the course of the discussion. He may not have secured the perfect method of dealing with his country's ills, but he cer-

---

[4] Ssu-ma Kuang, 1019–1086. One of the greatest of Chinese historians and leader of the opposition to Wang An-shih. [Editor's note]

tainly set to work in sincere and practical fashion to find a remedy for them.

Possibly Ssu Ma Kuang meant that Wang's policy was "idealistic" and therefore "impracticable." Critics often refer to Wang An Shih's theories as "unusual," "utopian," and the like. Liang Ch'i Ch'ao says that his measures were closely akin to those advocated by State socialists, and such as modern governments find extremely difficult to carry out. Certainly when one considers the vast extent of the Chinese empire, the lack of communications, the ignorance of the people on matters political, and other features characteristic of the empire nearly a thousand years ago, this experiment of Wang An Shih may be classed as "idealistic" in character. But it is not on that ground to be regarded as "impracticable." For, as we shall see, in spite of all the difficulties that have been enumerated, a certain measure of success attended his efforts. Further, if only his political opponents had maintained those features which the trial period of Shen Tsung's reign had shown to be both "practicable" and "advantageous," eliminating only those points which experience had shown to be either "impracticable" or "deleterious," it is quite probable that a permanent contribution of great value would have been made toward the solution of the economic problems of the Chinese people.

Holcombe asserts that "basically, the ills of China are of an economic character." [5] It is true that in Wang An Shih's day, the chief question facing the mind of any serious statesman was the economic condition of the country. We have shown that the national budget was showing a serious deficit every year, that the government officials were poorly paid, and that the aggressive tactics of border foes called for ever increasing expenditure on the military forces of the empire. In such circumstances it was inevitable that a man of Wang An Shih's character should devote prime attention to financial and military matters. Chu Hsi makes this to be his great crime, but

[5] *The Chinese Revolution,* by A. N. Holcombe.

when all the factors of his times are taken into consideration, the fact that he did so is greatly to his credit.

Let us now examine his method of dealing with the basic problem, namely, that of finance. His great object was to provide the government with increased revenue. According to Ssu Ma Kuang the only way to do this was to increase the taxation of the people. Against this Wang An Shih proposed his theory that the revenue could be increased without adding to the burdens of the people. Although this seemed to Ssu Ma Kuang "impracticable" and "unheard of," Wang An Shih proceeded to demonstrate its eminent "practicability."

The obvious thing to suggest in a time of national financial stringency is "economy." This naturally appealed to Wang An Shih and his political opponents alike as one way out of their difficulties. But while men like Ssu Ma Kuang were content with the suggestion, and with pointing out the difficulty of making any substantial reductions immediately, Wang An Shih got to work, and actually effected considerable reductions in a very short space of time. For this Shen Tsung must take a share of the credit, for the reduction on the national budget was effected largely, if not altogether, on the various items under the heading of Court expenditure.

Another method which suggested itself, and which to some extent Wang An Shih adopted, was to increase the revenue by enlarging the borders of the Imperial territory, thereby adding to the population of the empire, and naturally increasing the revenues by extending the poll-tax to larger numbers. Concurrently it was hoped that the area of arable land would be greatly extended by schemes of colonization of the border territories in the north-west. Tribes of the south and west which had so far maintained their economic independence he sought to bring under the authority of the Imperial Court, and impose regular taxation upon them. These objects were all included in his military policy.

Economy, however, could only be regarded as a minor expedient, and there were obvious limits to the possibilities of extending the national territory. Wang An Shih had something more fundamental and permanent to suggest for increasing the revenues. He felt that the resources of the country could be increased. Ssu Ma Kuang had said that this was impossible, that the available resources had already been fully exploited, and divided between the people and the government in due proportion. So that as he saw it, any addition to the government's portion would mean a deprivation of the people's share, which would be inimical to their livelihood.

Wang An Shih, however, proceeded to demonstrate that the government could increase its revenues without injury to the livelihood of the people; in fact his method was to increase the productive capacity of the people, so as to improve their livelihood on the one hand and add to the government revenues on the other. . . .

Commerce and agriculture were the two great national assets of the time, and it was to these that Wang An Shih gave prime attention. The small trader represented the great bulk of the merchant population. Wang An Shih by the promulgation of the "Trade and Barter Measure" [6] sought to free these from disabilities such as the accumulation of stocks represented by buying these up in the name of the government. In this way he hoped to encourage increased production, and effect a better trade situation. In addition, by the loan system which was a part of this measure, he sought to help them to continue production in times of difficulty. For by this system they were offered loan facilities at much lower rates of interest than they would have to pay normally to the money-lenders.

Further, he encouraged trade with the border tribes by his scheme of colonization in the north-west, and by the lifting of the embargo on the export of copper. These were all measures designed to increase the financial resources of the empire.

For the farmers, whose livelihood and

[6] State Trade System. [Editor's note]

economic prosperity was still more vital to his programme, he devised many schemes. His Agricultural Loans Measure [7] was intended not only to relieve the farming class of the intolerable burden of interest which the callous money-lenders exacted of them in difficult times, but also to ensure that the work of agriculture should be regularly conducted without such hindrances as lack of capital involved. His irrigation projects, and measures for river control, were designed to ensure an adequate water supply on the one hand, and to prevent flooding on the other. In this way also large tracts of land would be reclaimed and brought under the plough. The farming class was helped in other ways too. His Public Services Act [8] exempted the lower classes (of whom the farmers formed the great bulk) from the exactions of the old Labour Conscription Acts. They were thus able to devote themselves more thoroughly and regularly to their work on the fields.

These, too, were methods of increasing the nation's resources.

In other directions, a saving of expenditure was brought about, thus increasing the revenue at the disposal of the government. His "Equitable Transport Measure" [9] was designed to save the heavy expenditure on conveying the tribute grain from the distant parts of the empire, and he prevented great losses on the actual transport of grain by employing merchant boats in competition with the Government Transport Services. Reference has been made to the economy he made on Court expenditure. His Militia Act [10] aimed at the reduction of the regular army with correspondingly less expenditure on the same, while at the same time providing for the training of far greater numbers of militia to take their place.

Then his various taxation measures were all devised with a view to increasing revenue. The great object of his "Equitable

[7] Farming Loans. [Editor's note]
[8] Hired-Services System. [Editor's note]
[9] Tribute Transport and Distribution System. [Editor's note]
[10] *Pao-chia* System. [Editor's note]

Land Tax Measure" [11] was that all land from which taxation could legitimately be derived should be made subject to taxation, while at the same time ensuring that taxation should be fairly apportioned according to the relative productivity of the land. His Public Services Act aimed at a more equitable assessment of the people, bringing many classes under the Act who had hitherto been exempt, and ensuring that those who could pay did pay proportionately to their financial assets, while those who were too poor to contribute to the national exchequer were relieved of their responsibility for so doing.

From this brief sketch of his economic policy it will be seen that in aim, at least, the measures devised leave nothing to be desired. Each was definitely constructive, in that either economy or increased productivity was the objective in each case. The only classes who were called upon to pay increased levies were the wealthy, whom he conceived as having been too leniently dealt with hitherto, whereas the measures were uniformly devised for the relief of the poorer classes. So interpreted they were equitable, and even beneficent, as well as efficient measures of finance, and Wang An Shih may be considered to have justified his contention that there were ways of increasing the revenue without increasing the taxation. His economic policy, as far as its aim is concerned, we may then pronounce sound and good.

But that is not sufficient. We must examine the measures in their actual operation and investigate their effect before pronouncing final judgment upon them. If Chu Hsi is correct, these very measures were deemed cruel and oppressive, so much so that the people clamoured to be saved from them, as they had deprived them of all joy in life.

It is necessary, therefore, that this statement should be fully examined as to its truth or falsity, and with that in view it will be desirable to look at each of the

[11] Land Survey and Equitable Tax. [Editor's note]

Measures in detail, first investigating the nature and implications of the measures, and then endeavouring to estimate the value of each in actual results as far as such are ascertainable, allowing room in our judgment for the opinions of important critics of a contemporary and later age.

We will begin with the Public Services Act. This was devised with the idea of abolishing the old system of Labour Conscription for State services which had hitherto been operative, and supplanting it by a system of paid labour for all types of public work. The funds for this were to be gained from taxation according to property qualification, the poorer classes being entirely exempt from taxation on this account. It partakes of the nature of the Income Tax Measure so common in Western countries at the present day. As such it must have been welcome to the poorer classes at least, for not only were they exempted from taxation in connection with it, but all the services which they might be called upon to render for the officials were to be paid for. Under the older Labour Conscription Act the poorer classes would have been called upon at the whim of the local official for such services as road-making, dyke construction, porterage and transport, escorting, the work of servants, doorkeepers, scavengers, and the like. The demands of the public services did not always coincide with the needs of agriculture, and doubtless much interference with farming pursuits resulted, in addition to the fact that no pay could be expected. The poorer classes, then, ought to have had no reason for complaining that this measure operated in any oppressive way.

The middle and higher classes under the old Conscription Act had been liable for services of a clerical, commercial, financial, and administrative character. They had either undertaken these themselves, or had hired others to do the work for them. But it was their responsibility, and not only did they receive no certain remuneration for this work, but they were often involved in heavy financial losses. Under the Public Services Act these classes provided a definite sum of money for the maintenance of these services, and they themselves were eligible to receive the remuneration for such work which was now provided for by the Act of Wang An Shih.

It is conceivable that even these classes were better off under this Act than under the old one. In fact Ssu Ma Kuang said that the richer classes were better off under this Act than they had been under the old, and that was a reason why in his opinion it should be abrogated. Tseng Pu affirmed that all classes were better off, if the hitherto exempted classes were excepted.

In all probability the real "grouse" about this measure came from this hitherto privileged section of the populace. It will be remembered that under the old Conscription Act, officials, priests, and families with one male member, or none, had been exempted from all liability for the public services. Under the new Act of Wang An Shih, all these were brought within the meaning of the Act, provided that their property qualification demanded it. These were, as one critic pointed out, the class who could make themselves heard. Especially in the case of the officials was this true. Wang An Shih was also warned that once this proposal became law, the local officials would be deprived of their most powerful instrument of intimidation and graft. It is only natural to expect that the officials, who had hitherto been exempt from paying this tax themselves and who were being deprived of their most lucrative medium of "graft," should find the new Act inconvenient, and raise their voices in protest.

As regards the priests, these were usually attached to temples and monasteries, which possessed "glebe-lands" and received considerable income from gifts of devotees and local residents. Their quota would doubtless come from these sources, and little hardship would be experienced by them. The families with only one male member or with no male at all would only be taxed if their financial standing rendered them liable. So looking at this Measure all round, it is difficult to see where it could be termed oppressive or injurious.

Against the testimony of Ssu Ma Kuang, that the Measure operated to the detriment of the poorer classes, we can place the witness of Su Shih and Su Che, who after ten years of actual experiment, protested strongly against the abrogation of the new Measure. The evidence of these two is all the stronger from the fact that both had formerly been powerful advocates of Labour Conscription. Now the former was prepared to say that "even a sage could not improve upon the hiring system."

The only points they could urge against it were that money was being collected in excess of the actual needs of the public services in the various districts, and that city residents were being asked for more than their legitimate share. It was urged that half the rates charged should have sufficed. In this, as in other Measures where collections from the people were to be made by local officials, it is probable that malpractice occurred, and that if the Measure was operated in any way detrimentally to the livelihood of the people, it would be due to the character of the local officials rather than to the intrinsic character of the Measure itself.

The other great criticism levelled against this Measure was that paid agents of the government, like police and those in charge of public funds, etc., would of necessity prove unreliable. But there was plenty of testimony on the other side. Moreover, one of the provisions of the Act was that guarantors should be found for all who were holding responsible positions.

Ssu Ma Kuang also made much of the point that under the New Measure certain classes were taxed which had formerly been exempt. He must have been referring to city residents of the fourth and fifth classes. It does not follow, however, that the Measure was oppressive on that account. It should also be noted that when Ssu Ma Kuang revived the Labour Conscription

Measure he retained certain features of Wang An Shih's Act, such as the "Aid Money," payment of Official Agents, and permitting those classes liable for services who could afford it to hire substitutes.

Taking this Measure as a whole, it would seem to have been generally acceptable and beneficial. The salaries of officials were increased by it, while the numbers of farmers employed on public works were considerably reduced. This freed greater numbers for agriculture. Further, considerable revenue accrued to the government, while at the same time the public services were efficiently maintained. It was financially sound and ethically just. What more can be expected of a political measure?

It was the abrogation of this particular Measure by Ssu Ma Kuang which caused Wang An Shih most grief. He felt that this Measure at least ought not to have been rescinded.

The Agricultural Loans Measure was designed to help the farmer to tide over the spring season, when his resources were usually getting low. Formerly they contracted loans with the money-lenders at exorbitant rates, or refrained from doing so, in which case their fields were allowed to lie fallow, and they were compelled to face the prospect of no crops and consequent poverty. From the farmer's point of view, this Measure should have been most welcome. It is true they had to pay interest to the government instead of to the money-lender, but the rate was definitely fixed at 24 per cent per annum, which was considerably less than they would have had to pay to others.

Wang An Shih affirmed that the government expected no revenue from the working of these loans, but that it was impossible to work the Measure without this amount of interest, as this was required to meet the salaries of officials engaged and other expenses.

This Measure, however, was fruitful of great criticism and opposition on the part of prominent officials of the time. Han

Wei Kung[12] and Ou Yang Hsiu pointed out certain defects in its operation, and the latter refused to distribute the loans in his own district of Ch'ing Chow Fu. The main ground of their opposition seemed to be that the local officials in charge of the Measure were compelling people to take the loans against their will. Compulsion of this sort was prohibited by the government, but one can readily perceive that it was impossible to make such prohibition effective.

There was also allowance for reduction of the interest on the loans in poor years, and for the distribution of free relief in times of absolute dearth. But it was pointed out by critics that the officials would in such cases compel the people to take out further loans instead of granting these privileges, and that led to the piling up of debts which they could not possibly repay.

Wang An Shih, in his memorial on Five Matters, emphasized the dangers inherent in the working of this Measure, chiefly on the ground that the officials would not administer it according to his own ideas. Evidently this was the main cause of opposition. It must not be forgotten that Li Ts'an had administered the Measure successfully in Shensi, and Wang An Shih had certainly carried out the idea in Chin Hsien to the great gratification of the people.

Another difficulty pointed out by critics in connection with this measure was doubtless very real, namely that the poor people were only too ready to contract the loans, but not so ready to repay. This had led to the system of demanding guarantors from the local gentry, who naturally resented having to pay up considerable sums for absconding neighbours.

But evidently the greatest cause for objection, which could probably be substantiated, was the compelling of people to take loans against their will, and for this the local officials were again responsible.

[12] Han Wei Kung. Perhaps this is Han Wei, the early patron and later opponent of Wang An-shih. [Editor's note]

It was considered creditable for them to disburse large sums, and they were only too keen to get the "kudos" which would accrue from such "success."

There are, however, many things to be urged in favour of the Measure, and many witnesses can be produced in evidence of its popularity and successful working.

There is the testimony of Wang Kuang Lien, transport officer of Ho Pei, that "all the people are not only pleased but grateful," and that of Li Ting, who said that the people in the south were all gratified by its promulgation. There is evidence from Wang An Shih's own correspondence that the people welcomed the Measure and that success had attended its operation. He wrote to Tseng Kung Li that "it was thought that the people would not ask for the loans, but it was found that they welcomed the opportunity to do so." To quote again his memorial on Five Matters, he writes: "Of old the poor paid interest to the money-lenders, but now they pay to the officials. The latter demand lighter rates of interest, and the people are thereby saved much distress." Again, in a letter written to Shen Tsung after Wang An Shih had retired from office at the capital, he writes, "We prepared the Measure most carefully before promulgating it, and despite much criticism we may be said to have attained to success."

Such criticisms as these, however, may justly be discounted as coming either from members of Wang An Shih's own party or from the promoters of the Measure.

Fortunately, criticism of a favourable character from other sources is available. Take the following quotation from Chu Hsi, found in his work, the "Chin Hua She Ts'ang Chi":

After an investigation into the opinions of former worthies, and looking at the matter also from the standpoint of a modern critic, who has experimented with it, I am bound to admit that the idea of the Agricultural Loans Measure cannot be termed "bad." It was, however, faulty in that money was distributed instead of grain; that the distribution centres were confined to the "hsien" and not set up in the villages; that it was administered by the government officials solely, and not in co-operation with the local residents; and that the aim before the promoters was to accumulate profits as quickly as possible, instead of being chiefly concerned with the welfare of the people.

This accounts for the fact that Wang An Shih could administer it successfully in one "hsien" and yet failed to administer it successfully throughout the empire. The fact that the measure had good possibilities accounts for the further fact that my master, Ch'eng Tzu, who at first severely criticized it, was later on compelled to change his mind, and came to regret his extreme utterances on the subject.

For the moment we will confine ourselves to the change of mind on the part of Ch'eng Hao,[13] which is extremely important, inasmuch as it represents the conversion of one of the most extreme critics of the Measure in Wang An Shih's time. For he had then written, "It is impossible to carry into effect a measure which everyone regards as impracticable." Later on, on Chu Hsi's evidence, he had come to regret such utterances. This must have been because he had come to see that the Measure after all was practicable, and that it had within it the possibilities of successful and beneficent operation.

We shall deal with Chu Hsi's own criticism later on.

When Ssu Ma Kuang came into power he abrogated the Agricultural Loans Measure in the 2nd month of 1086. But in the very next month Fan Ch'un Jen appealed for its restoration, on the ground that the national exchequer was depleted. This would suggest that the Measure was regarded by him as being at least profitable to the government. This was contrary to the intention of Wang An Shih, as we have observed, but indicates that in the end it worked out that way.

But what is more significant is that Ssu Ma Kuang himself, in the 8th month of

---

[13] I.e. Ch'eng Tzu above.

1086, affirmed in a memorial that "the great idea of the Agricultural Loans Measure was in the interests of the people, and all that was necessary (to make it successful) was that compulsory practices in connection with its administration should be prohibited."

Such a change of front on the part of these most prominent opponents of the Measure in Wang An Shih's day, after the lapse of seventeen or eighteen years, must have occurred because the Measure had proved itself to be beneficial.

Let us turn now to the criticism of Chu Hsi. He affirms that the idea of the Measure was good. As a matter of fact he himself initiated a similar Measure during his term of office in Ts'ung An Hsien, in the prefecture of Chien Ning. This he affirmed was based on the She Ts'ang Fa of the Chow and T'ang Dynasties, but that during the long period which had elapsed since the inauguration of the Measure, certain defects had arisen, particularly in regard to the fact that the people in the remote places could not take advantage of any distribution which was made, as the distributing centres were located in the "Hsien" and "Chow" cities only. Further, the laws connected with the Measure were so strict that the local officials were unwilling to go to the trouble of opening the granaries even in famine times. The result was that the grain gradually deteriorated, so that when the officials were compelled through force of circumstances to break the seals, they found the grain unsuitable for human consumption.

These defects he considered could be remedied by his own scheme, which he had put into effect in his own district, as follows:

In 1168 he had organized a "She Ts'ang" or Loan Granary, initiating the scheme with a gift of six hundred piculs from the government. This grain, he as official, together with two local gentry, had undertaken to distribute by way of relieving the distress of the people . . . on which they had secured permission to charge 24 per cent interest, to be repaid in grain. . . . In times of dearth the rate of interest would be reduced by half, and in times of absolute famine the grain would be distributed free.

He affirmed that after fourteen years of operation on these lines, the original loan of 600 piculs had been returned to the government, and that in addition they had in stock 3,100 piculs which had been accumulated out of the interest paid on the loans.

At this juncture, as there was such a large stock in hand, he proposed that the procedure should be continued, but that the interest might be greatly reduced, only 3 per cent being demanded. He suggested, however, that lay residents should be put in charge, and that they should be under the inspection of the officials.

In conclusion, he affirmed that such a procedure was of permanent benefit, both to the government and the people, "and recommended that it should be applied universally."

This, on the one hand, is adequate testimony to the practicability and benefit of such a measure, and on the other serves to indicate the reasons for such lack of success as attended the efforts of Wang An Shih in connection with it. Chu Hsi states that under the provisions of Wang's Measure money was distributed instead of grain. This would undoubtedly arouse the cupidity of some people. Also in pointing out that the distribution centres were too few, and that the people who most needed the loans were by their remoteness from the centres unable to take full advantage of the Measure, and also in suggesting that local residents should be asked to cooperate in the administration of the scheme, he has probably indicated the weak points in Wang An Shih's Measure. For in keeping the distribution of the loans in the hands of the officials, it was impossible on the one hand to create as many centres as were essential to the efficient working of the Measure, and it was inevitable on the other that malpractices should arise.

Had all the officials of the "hsiens" been of the same calibre as Wang An Shih or the circuit officials of equal character and ability as Li Ts'an, no doubt the Measure would have worked satisfactorily to all concerned. For it might have been possible after the lapse of several years to reduce the rates of interest, which, after all allowances have been made, were still too high to enable the farmers to derive any great and permanent benefit from the loans. But Wang An Shih thought it essential that officials should be used for the work, and that in accordance with his policy of centralization of authority, it was necessary for the government to control the administration of the Measure. Had he gone the further step, which was taken by Chu Hsi, of enlisting local gentry of repute to supervise the actual working of the Measure, using the officials for inspection purposes only, it would have been unnecessary to charge such a high rate of interest.

However, that is criticism of a *post hoc* character, and we must not lose sight of his difficulties. He was in office for a comparatively short period of nine years, the country was vast, and communications were difficult. It was impossible to alter the character of the officials in that short space of time. He was opposed, in many cases, most unreasonably by the more famous officials of the time, and lost the support and prestige which their cooperation would have given to him. His own statement of the purpose of this Measure must be given due weight, viz., "we have the repression of the rich, and the relief of the poor in mind." In these respects at least he succeeded, and although his success was but relative, the Measure had in it the possibility of real and permanent worth.

When Chu Hsi was criticized for adopting a Measure which was an imitation of this particular Act of Wang An Shih, he replied, "But this was the only good measure Wang An Shih introduced."

As to the implication of the last clause, we naturally reserve judgment, but it serves to show that Chu Hsi thought this measure at least was a good one.

Liang Ch'i Ch'ao's criticism of this Measure is that as it involved the government in direct banking transactions with the people, it was so far faulty. But he gives Wang An Shih full credit for perceiving that something in the nature of a government bank was essential to all industrial and banking enterprise of a private character.

Our own judgment is that in view of the times, and taking the nature of his difficulties into account, Wang An Shih devised a very creditable measure for the relief of the poor and the repression of the rich. If he had been longer in office he would gradually have adapted the measure so as to make it of permanent and universal benefit. The measure operated beneficially to the poor, comparatively speaking that is, but aroused the opposition of the wealthy, who objected to being compelled to accept loans, for which they had no need. That they were so compelled was due to the character of the officials operating the measure, and not to the character of the measure itself.

"The Equitable Transport Measure," "Reformed Transport Measure," and the "National Trade and Barter Measure" may conveniently be considered together.

The objects of the first are clearly stated by Wang An Shih himself, viz., "The control of prices and the collection and distribution of the nation's resources will be more fully controlled by the government. Dearth and surplus will be mutually adjusted. Transport will be more economically managed, and greater efficiency secured. This will tend to eliminate burdensome taxation and the farming class will be proportionately relieved. In these ways it is conceivable that the government revenue will be adequately provided for, and the resources of the people suffer no serious injury."

Evidently this Measure was promulgated primarily with a view to reducing the expenses of collecting and transporting the grain which was contributed by the people as taxes. By giving the Transport Officers a capital sum, and giving them liberty to buy and sell according to varying conditions, and transporting Court supplies from as near as possible to the capital, it was thought that many other advantages such as are outlined above would accrue.

As, however, the Measure also permitted the exchange of other commodities which the Court might require, and as also the operation of the Measure tended to put the control of prices into the hands of the government, the Measure gradually called into existence a form of National Sale and Barter agency for all kinds of goods. The "Equitable Transport Measure" operated for a very short period, being merged into the "National Trade and Barter Measure," of which we must now speak.

This Measure gradually evolved out of attempts to solve certain practical problems, originating with Wang Shao's[14] scheme for colonization of the north-west, and his endeavour to establish improved trade relationships with the alien tribes inhabiting the border territory. The government was to establish trade stations, and finance them, in convenient places along the borders, exchanging, purchasing, or selling goods as they had opportunity. Prices would be fixed by the government. Later on the profits accruing from this business were to be devoted to the colonization of the territory with Chinese citizens, bringing the land under the plough, and offering a wider field for commercial activities. The national revenue would thereby be supplemented.

Later again, the idea of the scheme was extended to the capital, and branches set up in all important centres throughout the empire. As thus extended in scope it aimed chiefly at the relief of the small trader, who hitherto could only dispose of his surplus stocks to the wealthy trade combines who offered whatever prices suited them, whereas under the provisions of the new Act

[14] Wang Shao. An official who in 1070 apparently originated the idea developed by Wang An-shih into the State Trade System. [Editor's note]

the government would purchase these surplus stocks at more equitable rates. The people were also permitted to make exchanges of goods at will, and even contract loans. This again furthered the tendency for the control of market prices to pass into the hands of the government, and for the State gradually to become the one big trade monopoly.

Criticism of this Measure was mainly of two kinds, one that it was beneath the dignity of the State to engage in the sale and barter of such goods as ice, coal, fruits, etc., and the other that it was detrimental to the people's livelihood. By the "people" must have been meant the "big trade combines," at whose profit-making proclivities the Measure was largely aimed. Undoubtedly it must have caused great trouble and necessitated a huge body of officials to deal with such matters.

However, Wang An Shih's reply to these criticisms was probably justified. He said, "The Trade and Barter Measure has been drawn up with the utmost care, with a view to removing long-standing difficulties connected with the people's livelihood, and also with the idea of eliminating the baneful influences of the wealthy and monopolist classes. No financial advantage accrues to the government from it."

So that in essence and aim it was another measure designed to relieve the small trader and curb the activities of the wealthy.

The main reason urged for its rescindment in the 12th month of 1085 was that no profit had been gained by the government out of it, so that in this respect at least Wang An Shih's contention was justified.

Liang Ch'i Ch'ao terms this the least satisfactory of Wang An Shih's measures. He credits him with having a good and beneficent ideal in devising it, but considers that it was essentially defective in that it combined banking and trade under the auspices of the government. He considers that banking belongs essentially to the sphere of private enterprise, although he admits that some sort of government supervision is necessary. For the first part of this contention he has the support of Mr. Baldwin,[15] the present leader of the British Conservative party, who is reported to have expressed himself recently as follows:

The fundamental conception of doctrinaire Socialism is that the State should have a virtual monopoly of spending. From this conception it is a short step to the advocacy of the control of banking by a public corporation. . . . But in the formation of those central banks, which have done so much to reconstruct the shattered, and to launch the new countries of Europe, the cardinal principle has been to complete the divorce of banking from government control.

This divorce of control Mr. Baldwin terms financial orthodoxy, and considers it of solid advantage to the people generally. His objection to government monopoly of banking would seem to be that a government might be tempted to adopt a financial policy dictated by other than purely financial considerations.

Liang Ch'i Ch'ao, while objecting to government monopoly of banking, which he considers was involved in this measure of Wang An Shih, yet gives him credit for perceiving that in this vital matter of national economic policy, some sort of government control of banking was necessary.

His second objection to the measure is that eventually it was bound to defeat the very object for which it was devised. Ostensibly it was inaugurated to fight private banking and trade monopolies, but in effect it tended to make the government the sole trade and banking monopoly. So that private commercial enterprise he considers was bound to suffer rather than prosper from its operation.

Another aspect of the Measure was that prices of all commodities should be fixed by the government. Of which the criticism of Lancelot Lawton with regard to Stalin's policy is apposite. He writes, "It was one of Stalin's ideas that all produce was to be

taken over by the State at fixed prices. Past experience shows that such prices will always be determined, not by economic principles, but by the financial straits of the government."

This is not the place to enter upon a discussion of the tenets of State Socialism. The criticism of this particular measure from that angle must be left to abler minds. The idea of the writer is that Wang An Shih did not foresee the development of this State and Barter Measure into what was virtually a State monopoly of banking and commerce. From other writings on the subject of State monopolies we gather that in principle Wang An Shih was opposed to all such. His prime object in devising this measure was to relieve the small trader of surplus stocks, and to encourage continued and increased production. He had as secondary object the relief of such from the depredations of the professional moneylenders. Also in attempting to fix the prices of all commodities he was seeking to prevent the trade combines from fleecing the people, and taking advantage of times of dearth and emergency to exact extravagant profits. From a scheme of colonization and the attempt to improve relations with the border tribes, through an experiment to relieve the small trader of serious disabilities, the measure gradually developed far beyond the intention of Wang An Shih, and became contradictory of it. It would seem that this measure, while definitely beneficent in aim, turned out to be economically unsound. . . .

With the whole of Wang An Shih's fiscal policy before us, certain things can definitely be said. He had the interests of the poorer classes at heart. One fails to see any sign of "oppression" in his policy. "Repression" of the profiteering proclivities of the capitalists there certainly was. Deprivation of certain hoary privileges which the official and wealthier sections of the community had hitherto enjoyed, was a characteristic of his policy, but that can hardly be termed "oppression."

He was out to redistribute the wealth of

[15] Mr. Baldwin. Stanley Baldwin, 1867–1947. [Editor's note]

the country more equitably. He took from the rich to relieve the poor. He was determined to increase the national revenues, but he did this not by grinding the faces of the poor, but by taking more from those who could well afford to pay. As Dr. Ferguson says, "While Wang An Shih laid great stress upon the foundations of prosperity being in the increased wealth of the nation, yet his intense sympathy with the people, and his anxiety for their welfare, ennobled all his plans with a high standard of moral worth."

In aim he was sincere and his measures were devised with beneficent objects. Those who suffered from his economic policy were the "privileged" and influential sections of the populace. These were naturally more "articulate" than others, and so in the accounts which have come down to us, the side of the case which they represent is emphasized in such a way as to give the impression that his measures were "oppressive." If the poorer classes suffered at all from his policy, it was not due to anything inherent in the measures themselves, but to the way in which they were administered by the local officials, whose "acquisitive" tendencies, "love of wealth and fame" were ingrained in their very natures.

If it be urged, as indeed some critics have done, that Wang An Shih failed to make full allowance for this, and that therefore he is culpable, the same argument applies to any other minister who should attempt to introduce any financial measure at all. If Wang An Shih's reforms failed because the local officials were corrupt, then even the old system of government must have been working at least equally badly. It is suggested that Wang An Shih and his party thought that by paying the officials more, their self-respect would be enhanced and they would not be so prone to follow corrupt practices. "But," laments Chu Hsi, "they still continued their dishonest ways."

So that whatever criticism may be applied to Wang An Shih in this connection, applies equally to every other attempt at reform made during that age, whether conservative or liberal in character.

The Militia Act and the Militia Mounts Measure were also part of his economic policy in certain respects, but as they were primarily concerned with the military situation, we have not discussed them under the head of his fiscal programme. But it must be remembered that in seeking to reduce the regular forces and replace them with voluntary or civil levies, without increasing the military expenditure on the normal budget, and at the same time actually increasing the military force at the disposal of the government, the measures had their definite place in his economic policy.

It has already been pointed out that the threatened invasion from the Tartars in the north and the Tanguts in the northwest determined Wang An Shih's military policy to a large degree, and that it was definitely with the idea of coping with that threat that these two measures were devised.

The condition of the regular forces can be gauged from the criticism of such men as Ou Yang Hsiu, Fan Chen, and Su Shih, none of whom can be considered friendly toward Wang An Shih's policy in general. The former termed the standing forces "a mere pretence of an army" and severely criticized their arrogance, indolence, and ineffectiveness. Fan Chen said that the regulars were quite useless as a fighting force, and that the enormous number enrolled acted deleteriously to agriculture, by drafting off those who should have been at work on the fields. He considered some system of people's levies and the revival of the soldier-farmer policy essential. Su Shih said the 50 per cent of the regular forces might be disbanded without doing the State any injury, as through age or physical incapacity quite that proportion were useless.

So disbandment of large numbers of regulars was one of the chief features of Wang An Shih's military policy. He was aware, however, of the danger of doing this too hastily, and emphasized the necessity of doing it in gradual fashion, urging in fact that large reductions could be effected without taking any drastic action at all, as considerable numbers left the army through various reasons, and all that was necessary was that these should not be replaced. The standing army at the opening of Shen Tsung's reign numbered 1,162,000 men, whereas at the time of Wang An Shih's retirement from the Grand Council there were only 568,688 on the roll. This was practically equivalent to the reduction of the 50 per cent which Su Shih had advocated.

His next step was to ensure that the disbanded regulars should be supplanted by corps raised from the people, who were to be drilled in the intervals between the agricultural seasons, provided with trained officers and weapons, and gradually rendered available, first for police duty locally, and eventually for actual warfare. It will be noted that the Measure gradually extended both in nature and scope, but that the original intention of its promoters was to get the people of the north and north-western districts trained first.

The expenses were to be secured from the Military Treasury, and in the main provided for by the saving on the regular army which the stopping of recruiting made possible.

By the year 1076 no less than 7,182,028 men were enrolled in the Militia.

In the appeal for abrogation which Ssu Ma Kuang made when he was restored to power, the points emphasized were the larger numbers enrolled, that the officials in charge of the measure were not keeping to the original conditions of the Act as promulgated, and that the people were being treated badly by those responsible for its administration. He urged further that agriculture was being interfered with, that the farmer forces would never become effective as a fighting force, and that the Measure would result in the increase of robbery and brigandage.

Wang Yen Sou quarrelled not so much with the Measure itself, as with the way in which it was being administered. The greater part of the people's dissatisfaction was caused by the character and practices of the officials in charge, who had no desire to benefit the country.

The numbers were of course huge, but the task before them was tremendous, and considering that the militia were to do duty as local police as well as be held in reserve for actual warfare, the numbers cannot be considered excessive. As regards interference with agriculture, we gather that at the most fifty days in the year were to be given to drill, which probably meant five days each month during ten months in the year. In many cases this was reduced to twenty-seven days and some even were called up for only eighteen days per annum. Complete exemption was possible in famine times or through other exceptional circumstances.

The men were of necessity called up in relays, and as agriculture has its definitely busy seasons, no doubt the two months which were excepted, would be the sowing and harvest seasons. For the rest of the year it is usually possible for the farmer to have his days off every month.

The character of the officials has of course to be taken into account, and while in intent and actual character the Measure may have been designed so as not to interfere with agriculture, it is extremely probable that in the actual carrying out of the Act such interference did occur. The officials would doubtless take advantage of the opportunity afforded by this Measure to use the people for work other than military drill, and no doubt bribery had to be resorted to in some cases to get free from their clutches.

As to the point of efficiency, we have the testimony of Chang Ch'un, who in regretting the abrogation of the Militia Act, said, in 1095, that the militia after training were superior to the regular forces. And still more powerful testimony is afforded by the word of Ssu Ma Kuang himself who, in attempting to supplant the Act by the older regulations for the Archers, said that in the militia a large body of well-trained men was available for this work.

Unfortunately there was no actual experiment made with the militia as a fighting force, so it is impossible to say from experience how the plan would have worked out from that point of view. The real spirit of the Measure was never restored after Ssu Ma Kuang's attempts at abrogation, and such offers as were made by men like Ch'in Yuan to lead the militia against the invading Chins were rejected.

But the contention of Ch'en Ju Ch'i that if the Militia Act had not been rescinded the invaders would have met with stout opposition seems justified. With this Liang Ch'i Ch'ao is in agreement.

Chu Hsi says it was Wang An Shih's plan to make this scheme fully effective throughout the empire, but that he did not succeed in doing so. He speaks approvingly of the idea, and commends one Fan Chung Ta for having carried out the idea splendidly in Yuan Chow.

It was, of course, a very difficult Measure to carry through, as the ordinary civilian population anywhere is naturally opposed to being called upon for regular periods of military training. In the case of this particular Measure not only was there that obstacle to override, but also the dissatisfaction of numbers of regulars who must have been disbanded, willy-nilly, through the operation of the Act. Add to that the large amount of opposition from official quarters, based largely on factious considerations, and it is remarkable that Wang An Shih made as much progress as he did with this Measure.

Liang Ch'i Ch'ao thinks the Militia Mounts Measure was unsatisfactory in that the people were compelled to replace diseased or dead mounts, and that it was wrong for the government to lay the burden of feeding the animals on the local population. Those are obvious defects, but against these must be put the facts that the people had the use of the animals, and that horses in sufficient quantity were not available in the national stud. Horses were essential for the use of the militia, and so

by force of circumstances he was induced to adopt the idea.

The whole plan was, of course, practically equivalent to the conscription of the available male forces of the empire for warfare. But as Wang An Shih had his face turned toward the ancient precedents, he could think only in terms of the ancient practices, and hence he failed to introduce conscription such as Western nations or the Japanese have devised, i.e. regular periods of two or three years with the army for all males. Justification for the attempt he made is to be found in the situation of his time, and evidently his fears and preparations were more than justified, for half a century later the whole of north China passed into the hands of the northern foe. So he should be given credit for realizing that a measure of compulsory military training was necessary and justifiable at that period. . . .

A full chapter has been devoted to Wang An Shih's educational policy, to which little can be added. He was evidently desirous of extending the school system of government education, and did something toward carrying his plans into effect. But his short term in high office prohibited the possibility of applying his ideas to the whole country. So perforce he had to be content with the revision of the examination system, by means of which the government officials were selected. By seeking to make the candidates concentrate on a method of classical study which tended to make them more practically minded, and so more useful in actual administration, he was making a very valuable contribution to the educational problems of his time.

The nature of the questions which he himself set at the official examination shows that he intended the candidates to think and not merely to rely upon their memories. Knowledge rather than style, thought rather than memory, and practical mindedness rather than literary skill were the features which he sought to introduce by his educational reforms.

The ancient bases of selection for government positions emphasized personal character, knowledge of the classical literature, government administration, and literary skill. It seems that Wang An Shih had all these in mind, and kept them in much the same order of relative importance. For he was always stressing the importance of personal character in the officials. "The keeping of the laws depends upon the officials. If the officials are of unworthy character, the laws, no matter how good and complete they may be in themselves, will not be kept." He thought the school system the best that could be devised for discovering the personal character of the official candidates, but until that method was available he thought that close investigation of their record and recommendation by worthy men were the best substitutes. The period of trial was also emphasized by him, a method which in name at least was already in vogue, but which he sought to make more effective by stressing the investigation side of a man's official record.

His actual work of reform on the National College or University was all in line with these broad principles. He extended the accommodation, increased the numbers of students in residence, offering especially greater facilities for students not of the official clan, and by adding to the curriculum such practical subjects as Law, Medicine, and Military knowledge he was seeking to impart that note of utility to education which he was ever stressing as being of first importance.

By limiting the sphere of study each year to one classic, he aimed at thoroughness, and by combining personal character with general learning in the grading of the men he was laying the emphasis in the right place.

One could have wished that he had had a longer period in which to extend his contribution to education. In the times of Chu Hsi the latter stressed almost identically the same points as Wang An Shih. "He deplored the lack of emphasis on personal character in the selection of officials in his day, and stressed the fact that this was the main object of the ancients in establishing their school system. He affirmed, too, that as the government school system had ceased to emphasize character, the educated class had perforce gone to the Buddhists and Taoists for religious and ethical conceptions, and that instead of making personal character the main criterion of a man's capacity for an administrative post, literary ability was regarded as of chief importance." All this might have been written by Wang An Shih himself, and serves to enhance the value of his own theories and contribution.

In the foregoing discussion we have endeavoured to give the reader some account of the motives which inspired Wang An Shih in embarking upon his career of political reform. We have also tried to indicate the aim he had in view in devising his various measures. These again have been outlined in some detail, the nature and value of each have been estimated in some degree, and some insight has been gained into his difficulties and the character of the opposition. We must now attempt to view his policy as a whole and seek to evaluate his political contribution in general.

The fact that the Emperor Shen Tsung maintained Wang An Shih's policy without any important change for the whole of his reign (1068–1085) is not without significance. It must be remembered that Wang An Shih resigned in 1076, so that for a period of nine years, although Wang An Shih was living in retirement, his policy was considered so satisfactory to the Emperor that he thought it unnecessary to introduce any serious modifications. It may, however, be urged that Shen Tsung's interest in the maintenance of Wang An Shih's policy may have been dictated by purely personal considerations, as he had been so intimately associated with his minister in the formulation of it. Further, in support of this it may be said, and justly, that the Emperor was first and foremost concerned with the securing of increased revenue and the creation of a more effective fighting force, and that these were the very things which Wang An Shih's policy was designed to produce. It is therefore only natural that the Emperor should maintain it without change. It may further be urged that mere maintenance of such a policy does not of necessity imply that it was beneficial to the people at large. Shen Tsung's interest in securing increased revenue might easily conflict with the welfare of the people, and the maintenance of a larger and more effective fighting force might be secured at the expense of the people's well-being.

Against such plausible arguments as these we would urge the following considerations.

Firstly, there is the account of Shen Tsung's character, as found in the Dynastic Histories, and which is quoted at the beginning of this chapter. A monarch who was keenly interested in the economic conditions under which the people lived, who was merciful to the poor and aged and generous to those in distress, could scarcely be willing to maintain a policy which "took away all joy in life," even though it happened to be a policy in which he was personally interested, as suggested above.

Secondly, there is no account in the Histories of the time of any serious uprising of the people against the measures introduced by Wang An Shih. As Liang Ch'i Ch'ao says, "If the people had been suffering hardships they would certainly have rebelled. For, under the provisions of the Militia Act, they were well organized and trained, and large numbers of them were provided with the weapons necessary for such a move.". . .

It would seem that at least the times of Shen Tsung's later reign were not such as Ssu Ma Kuang described when he said that the people dare not plant an extra mulberry or buy an extra cow for fear of being taxed out of existence.[16]

[16] Referring to the times of Ying Tsung. [Editor's note]

That, however, is evidence from Wang An Shih, and if it stood by itself might possibly be discounted. However, it is not to be ignored when supplemented by such witness as the following letter from Su Shih, a former opponent of the reform policy, written to his friend T'eng Ta Tao:

I should like to take the opportunity to talk over with you the way in which we showed our prejudices when the reform measures were under discussion, and how we were led to take up an opposing attitude. Although I feel that possibly at that time we thought we were acting sincerely and reached our position out of a real regard for the welfare of the country, I have now come to see that we were wrong and in the main unreasonable.

Now that the grace of the Emperor is constantly renewed, and his rule obviously successful, I perceive, looking back, that the attitude I then took up was far from what it should have been. Naturally one does not change one's point of view simply out of personal interest, or in order to enhance one's prestige and influence. I really do feel that unless we desist from our querulous opposition we shall take greater regrets than ever.

The testimony of this letter, that the rule of Shen Tsung was obviously successful, and other indications of a *volte face* on the part of so prominent an opponent of the reform policy as Su Shih, add considerable weight to the evidence already produced that Wang An Shih's measures could not have been acting in the oppressive manner suggested by Chu Hsi.

Other signs that Su Shih had changed his views on the reform policy are not lacking. For instance, it is recorded that during Wang An Shih's retirement at Chiang Ning, Su Shih visited him and that they enjoyed many pleasant rambles together in the surrounding hills.

There is evidence even from the school opposed both to Su Shih and Wang An Shih. Take for instance what Chu Hsi records about Ch'eng Hao's attitude to the Agricultural Loans Measure. He writes, "Although our master Ch'eng Tzu formerly criticized the measure severely, yet he could not avoid expressing his regrets later that he had been too extreme in his opposition." There are also the words of Ch'eng Hao himself that the unreasonable opposition of his party had driven Wang An Shih to proceed to extremes in his policy.

The fact that we have such evidence from the leaders of two of the great opposing parties to Wang An Shih's policy proves that there must have been many good features in it, sufficient at least to disprove Chu Hsi's contention that he pursued a policy of reckless and rigorous oppression. We do not hold a brief to prove the flawless character of Wang An Shih's administration. What has been said in our detailed discussion of the various measures is sufficient to show that. The new laws had their defects, and did not always or in every case work out in the best interests of the people. There were reasons for that, which we shall now proceed to discuss. But what we are at this point concerned to prove is that during the reign of Shen Tsung there was not the clamorous opposition on the part of the people which Chu Hsi's statement would lead us to believe. If there was clamorous opposition at all, it most probably emanated from the wealthier and more influential sections of the populace, who had many of their cherished privileges taken away by the operation of the new measures.

We have just suggested that the measures had their defects and that in some cases they were administered in such a way as to give just cause for resentment. We might venture to inquire into the reasons for that.

First as to the defective character of the measures themselves. This is attributed by Wang An Shih's critics to his depending too much upon his own knowledge and experience, upon his unwillingness to listen to the advice of others, upon his obstinacy, his unpractical mentality and the like. All of which, either openly or tacitly, assume that if he had subordinated his wilful ideas to the opinions of his so-called "loyal and worthy" contemporaries,

he would have produced much better measures and thereby avoided the opposition and enmity which proved so serious an obstacle to the success of his policy later on.

It is evident upon the face of it that for some reason or other Wang An Shih failed to secure the cooperation of those officials at Court whom posterity has regarded, justly in many cases, as able and honourable men. It is also quite reasonable to suppose that if he could somehow have enlisted their sympathetic cooperation, his reforms would have been more fruitful of beneficent and lasting results.

Chu Hsi, representing the opposition, attributes Wang An Shih's failure to secure this cooperation to his impetuosity and extreme self-confidence. He admits, however, that Wang An Shih had the right ideas for his day, and confesses that his critics failed to present sufficiently cogent reasons for their opposition, and that their alternative suggestions were nothing like so good as his proposals. He goes further, and says that he is not surprised that this made Wang An Shih more confident than ever that he had got the right way of doing things, and that it made him more than ever determined to carry out his own ideas. He blames Wang An Shih, however, for not having the patience to expound his ideas more fully. For if he had done so, instead of pressing them upon the Court with such arrogant self-assurance, the results would not have been so disastrous.

He says again, "When the new laws were first propounded, the loyal and worthy officials were sincerely desirous of cooperating, even Ch'eng Hao thinking it right to do so. That was because they perceived that such reforms as were suggested were called for by the nature of the times. However, when they found that they could not altogether approve of his ideas, Ch'eng Hao took it upon himself to remonstrate with Wang An Shih, exhorting him to desist from pursuing a course which was so obviously contrary to the general opinion. It was only after Wang An Shih had spurned the advice of the majority, and had made it quite obvious that he was going to push his own ideas with greater determination than ever, that the great body of worthy officials deserted the Court."

It is interesting to compare with this the opinion of Chang Ju Ming of the Ming Dynasty [1368–1644], who wrote an Introduction to Wang An Shih's works. He says, "Wang An Shih had the real interest of the State and the welfare of the people at heart. He had not even the vestige of self-interest. If only the great officials of his day could, out of sympathy with his real purpose, have given to his proposals the attention they deserved, or if only they could have admitted their good points and set themselves sincerely to remedy their defective features: If, again, they had only been broadminded enough and magnanimous enough to inquire about the matters which they did not fully understand, or if they had been willing to 'give and take' subduing their prejudices and desire for victory at any cost: If further they had been ready to cooperate with him with the sole purpose of seeking the good of their country, and helped him to find the right men to administer his measures, his policy would most assuredly have been of real and lasting value."

Chang Ju Ming cannot be regarded as unduly prejudiced in favour of Wang An Shih, for lower down, in this same Introduction, he refers to his lack of patience with the opposition, to a certain unreadiness to heed criticism, to his mistaken assumption that the opposition could be overcome by the exercise of disciplinary and punitive measures, and to his not being free from prejudices himself.

It seems to an observer, endeavouring to be impartial, that Wang An Shih's failure to secure the cooperation of the able and more famous men of his day was due to Wang An Shih's temperament on the one hand and the disposition of his opponents on the other! There is no doubt that he started out in the hope of cooperating with these talented and worthy men,

but that he found them extremely difficult to get on with. He had his strong mind, and they had their prejudices. He was a Radical, and they were inclined to be strongly Conservative. He had the ear of the Emperor, and this excited their envy and jealousy. He was perhaps a little too ready to dub them "conventional" and they were too ready to bark back and term him "bigoted." While admitting that there were faults on both sides, one's sympathy goes out to Wang An Shih, for he perceived that the nature of the times called for drastic and speedy action, and that the condition of the country was such that radical and far-reaching reforms were urgently needed. He was obviously sincere in his motives, as even his most doughty opponents are ready to admit; he had the right ideas for the times, as even Chu Hsi confesses. He had the confidence of the Emperor, and considerable influence over him. Both monarch and minister were out for the good of the country, and had constructive proposals to suggest. It was undoubtedly the duty of every right-minded and patriotic official to put up with Wang An Shih's idiosyncrasies and cooperate to the very utmost with him and their common ruler.

"But what were the facts?" continues Chang Ju Ming. "The publication of every new measure was accompanied by vituperous opposition. One day his opponents were denouncing him personally with the utmost vehemence, and the next vociferously decrying the character of the measure itself. The censors availed themselves of the opportunity this afforded to seek the reputation of a "courageous utterance," while the influential officials seized the opportunity to buy a name for "mercy" and sympathy with the people. The subordinate officials in the provinces flattered their patrons at Court by allying themselves with their particular faction. The result was that the Court "parliament" was transformed into a "bear-garden."

During all this fuss and palaver at the capital, no instance of the people making the character of the new measure a pretext for raising the flag of rebellion occurred, nor did the border tribes make them an occasion for unfriendly overtures.

Although everyone knew that the old methods of administration were imperfect, his opponents must of course decry the necessity of making any changes. Though the new measures met with their unequivocal denunciation, they were not of necessity deserving of it.

But how inconsistent many of his main opponents were! Ideas which they themselves had mooted earlier on they must perforce attack when Wang An Shih proposed them. Take for instance Su Che and his attitude to the Agricultural Loans Measure; Ssu Ma Kuang and the Public Services Measure; Su Shih in connection with the north-western policy, the Public Services Measure, and the Militia Act. Others like Han Ch'i and Ssu Ma Kuang opposed the Agricultural Loans Measure as being detrimental to the people's livelihood, but what alternative had they themselves to suggest for their relief?

Surely Wang An Shih had some justification for terming such opponents "conventional."

It seems inevitable in such circumstances that Wang An Shih should have taken things on to his own shoulders, although it is admittedly unfortunate that by so doing he lost the advice and the countenance which the support of these famous men would have given him.

Chu Hsi thinks that it was not the character of the measures so much as Wang An Shih's administration of them which made them deleterious, and that if Ch'eng Hao had headed them up the results would have been quite different. But he also says that Su Shih, if he had been given the scope that Wang An Shih had, would have made a much more disastrous job of things than *he* did. On the whole, one's opinion inclines to the view that considering all the circumstances Wang An Shih made an extremely creditable and valuable contribution.

As has just been suggested, Chu Hsi hints that the real fault lay not so much with the character of the measures as with the way in which they were administered. This brings us to the second suggested reason for failure, namely, the character of the men engaged on the actual prosecution of the reform policy. As to Wang An Shih's immediate associates, we have reached the conclusion that in the main they were quite good and able men. There were a few exceptions, as has been pointed out. But as far as the legislative side of things is concerned, little fault can be found with the character and the ability of the men engaged.

But when one considers the rapid and wide-sweeping changes which Wang An Shih introduced and the enormous number of subordinate officers that were required for the execution of them, it would have been surprising if there had been no occasion for complaint about the practical administration of the new laws.

Ts'ai Shang Hsiang[17] has a most apposite criticism in this connection. He says, "Wang An Shih had the right ideas for his day, but failed to discover the right method of carrying them out. He was able to supervise everything himself in a county district, and so made a great success of his political theories there. But when he tried to apply them to the whole country, he was naturally compelled to devolve responsibility on to a great number of others. These 'others' had not his spirit of conscientious responsibility nor his interest in the well-being of the people. They were covetous and unreliable. In thus failing to secure the right men, confusion and failure resulted."

The reasons for Wang An Shih's failure in this matter have been fully discussed in the chapter on his character, and need not be repeated here. Suffice it to say that such features as were deemed unjust or "oppres-

[17] Ts'ai Shang-hsiang was the Ch'ing dynasty scholar whose study of Wang An-shih and his reforms went to show that historical mistreatment had distorted the truth. His work opened the way for the modern reappraisal of Wang. [Editor's note]

sive" in the operation of his measures in his own day were all practically due to the character of the local officials administering them. Wang An Shih was fully alive to the danger of not securing the right men, especially when they had to administer such measures as he proposed. One of the great objects of his educational policy was to devise a method whereby the numbers of able and worthy officials might be greatly increased. But for the short time he was in power he was dependent upon such men as were available, and these, as Ts'ai Shang Hsiang points out, were far from being satisfactory. It was therefore Wang An Shih's misfortune rather than his fault that certain oppressive practices developed in the carrying out of his reform measures.

If in the actual drawing up of his measures he depended upon younger and less experienced men than the "old guard" of loyal and worthy officials represented, and thus failed to produce as perfect a series of reform laws as he might have done, then the "old guard" who deserted him must share the blame for the defects which the measures show. If the character of the local officials prevented the laws from functioning as fairly and beneficially as they might have done, then he may be said to have been unfortunate rather than blameworthy. For in such conditions no one could have done any better, probably not even Ch'eng Hao.

To sum up. It is admitted by friend and foe alike that Wang An Shih had the right ideas for his day, that the times called for such reforms as he proposed, and that he had the welfare of the country and the prosperity of the people generally as his aim. But the need for urgency on the one hand, and the clash of temperament between him and his political opponents, led him to push measures, which though in the main apposite and timely, were not without defects. These defective features arose through the limitations of one-party politics, but for this not only Wang An Shih is to blame. His political foes must share it. The character of the local officials accounts in the main for whatever was "unjust" or "oppressive" in the actual execution of the measures, and it is quite evident that these features were deplored equally by Wang An Shih and his opponents. Throughout his political career Wang An Shih aimed at the relief of the poorer classes and the more equitable sharing of the country's burdens by the classes most able to carry them. It was inevitable in these circumstances that he should meet with the enmity and opposition of the more influential classes, who were naturally more "vocal" than those whose cause he championed. So that in the historical records of the time, we read more of disapproval than approval of his policy. In addition to this general consideration we must not ignore the fact that the Histories were compiled by his political foes, and so still greater injustice is done to him in the records of the period.

Experiment in State Capitalism

LIN YUTANG

Lin Yutang (1894–   ), widely known as an essayist, interpreter of traditional Chinese ways of thought, and linguist, has been less frequently regarded
as a historian. He has often recorded his admiration of Taoist attitudes of
naturalness and simplicity in life and mistrust of excessively active government.
The selections below are taken from his biography of the poet Su Shih, or Su
Tung-p'o, for whom he feels a strong attraction. His concern with Wang
An-shih, whom his hero, Su Shih, opposed, may be viewed with these considerations in mind. If his judgment is not shared by most modern professional
historians, it nevertheless suggests the feeling that Wang An-shih is still
capable of rousing among Chinese interested in the history of their country.

WANG ANSHIH was a curious man, extraordinary in mind and character. He was an industrious student, a good scholar except in his abominable philology, and certainly a major poet. Unfortunately, he combined a Messianic sense of mission with a deplorable lack of tact and inability to get along with anyone but himself. He was at the same time unquestionably an impractical idealist. If by idealist we mean a man who was negligent of his food and appearance, Wang Anshih was certainly one. He achieved a certain notoriety by his dirty dress and his unshaved and unkempt appearance. Su Hsün characterized him in a rhetorical flourish as "dressed in a barbarian's robe and eating the food of pigs and dogs," and said that "he discussed history and poetry with a convict's unshaven head and unwashed face." Whether Wang Anshih loved that distinction or not we do not know, but it is easy to believe that a man so absorbed in his ideas was naturally negligent of his external looks. The story is told that he never changed his gown. One day some of his friends went with him to a bathhouse at a temple. The friends stealthily left a clean robe while he was in the bath and wanted to test whether he would find out his dress had been changed. Wang Anshih came out of his bath and put on the new robe, totally unaware of what his friends had done. Anyway, he had put on *a* robe.

Another day, his friends reported to Wang Anshih's fat wife that her husband loved shredded venison.

"I don't believe it," said his wife, greatly surprised. "He never pays any attention to his food. How could he suddenly love shredded venison? What makes you think so?"

"We know because at the dinner he did not take food from the other dishes, but finished all the shredded venison."

"But where did you put that dish?"

"Right in front of him," was the reply.

The wife understood, and said to his

friends: "I tell you what. You have some other kind of food put in front of him to-morrow and see what happens."

The friends, therefore, changed the position of the dishes the next day and put the shredded venison away from him and watched him eat. Wang Anshih began to take food from the dish next to him and did not know that the deer meat was upon the table.

The story is also recorded how Wang Anshih studied all night when he was serving on a magistrate's staff at Yangchow. The chief magistrate then was Han Ch'i, who later became premier. Wang would read all night and doze off in the chair toward dawn. On waking up he would find that he was late and then rush to the office without washing his face or combing his hair. Han Ch'i noted his appearance and, thinking that he had indulged himself all night with women, gave him a piece of advice.

"Young man," he said, "I should advise you to make the best use of the years of your youth and apply yourself to studies."

Wang Anshih stood there without giving any explanation, and on departing told his friends that Han Ch'i did not appreciate him. Later, as Wang's fame as a scholar steadily grew, Han changed his opinion of him and accepted him as a follower, which Wang rather resented. As it happened, the year Wang accepted a high office at the capital was the year in which Han Ch'i quit his office as prime minister. Wang also diligently kept a diary, running to seventy volumes, and in this diary he often put in the remark that "there is nothing to Han except his fine looks."

But there is more to this strange man than his unkempt appearance. For about two decades before his rise to power, what made him most talked about was his repeated refusal to accept promotion to an office at the court. It is hard to believe that he did this for the sole purpose of earning fame, for from his twenty-first year, when he passed the examinations, to his forty-sixth, when he came into power—that is,

during the most active years of his man-hood, a period of twenty-five years—he steadily declined appointments and always preferred to serve as a minor magistrate in the outlying provinces. It was during the reign of Jentsung, a very good period when all distinguished talents who could do so gathered at the court. The more Wang Anshih refused an offer of a good post, the more his fame grew. Finally it got to the point where all the officials at the court were dying to have a look at this man. For besides distinguishing himself by his liter-ary compositions, he had proved himself an able administrator as a magistrate. He had built dams, reformed schools, established loans for the farmers, and put into practice some of his new social ideas. It was a good administrative record and the people liked him. Enticements for him to come to the capital were without avail, and it was not until he was offered a job on the board of finance that he was attracted to the capital, in 1060. It is clear that this man was primarily interested in economics and finance and felt he could do most for the country along this line. Then his mother died and he had to retire; but even after the mourning period was over, when he was called to the court again, he refused the offer and remained away at Nanking.

This period of his self-imposed obscurity is difficult to understand, for the man cer-tainly believed that he had great things to do for the country when the time came, and it would have been logical for him to have built up his official career during the period of his manhood. Perhaps the competition of great scholars at the capital was too great for him, for there were certainly older, better, and sounder scholars, such as Fan Chungyen, Ssu-ma Kuang, Ouyang Hsiu, Tseng Kungliang, and others, who were in-clined to look askance at any radical re-forms and who commanded sufficient popu-lar prestige to discourage any young man with newfangled ideas. Wang Anshih bided his time. But I think psychologically there was another reason. A man of Wang's temperament had to be the boss wherever he was, and when serving as a magistrate in an outlying district, he was the big frog in a little puddle. Again and again, when he was in the capital holding some office for a short time, he quarreled with his colleagues and upset everything. He wanted to change the rules and run things in his own way. Wu K'uei and Chang Fangp'ing both recalled such experiences of difficult cooperation with him as a colleague or even as a junior official.

In 1060, therefore, he had come to the capital as a rather strange phenomenon. He had written good prose and poems. He had original ideas and was a good talker. The high-ranking old officials such as Fu Pi and Wen Yenpo had the best opinion of him, and even Ouyang Hsiu liked him. Here was a singular man beneath whose strange appearance lay talents and character the officials could not quite fathom. Among the few people who saw through Wang Anshih's character and considered him a great danger to the country were Su Hsün and his old friend Chang Fangp'ing. The latter had worked with him as a colleague in supervising certain local examinations, had dismissed him and never talked with him again. He must have told Su Hsün about his experiences with Wang in his early days. The two, therefore, intensely disliked Wang, the more for what they considered his affectations in dress and habits. Ouyang Hsiu had introduced Wang to Tungp'o's father, and Wang himself was desirous of making the acquaintance of the Sus, but Su senior refused to see him. When Wang's mother died, of all the invited guests, Su Hsün refused to attend the funeral and wrote the famous *Pien Chien Lun,* or "Essay on the Hypocrite," one of the most popular essays for school reading today.

In this essay Su Hsün started by pointing out how difficult it was to know a man's character and how often even clever people were deceived. Only the quiet observer could see through a man's character and foretell his future development. He quoted an ancient scholar who was able to foretell about Wang Yen when the latter was a brilliant young man distinguished for his appearance, and another great general who was able to foretell about Lu Ch'i, who was more or less responsible for bringing an end to the Tang dynasty. Lu Ch'i was a scheming person of great ability but so fearfully ugly that, in receiving him, the host had to dismiss all his female entertainers for fear that the women would be shocked or would offend him by ill-concealed titters. But, says Su Hsün, each of these separately would not have been enough of a personality to ruin an empire, had it not been for the weak-minded emperors under whom they came into power. Now, however, a man had appeared who combined the ugliness and scheming ability of a Lu Ch'i and the eloquence of a Wang Yen. "Here is a man who discourses on Confucius and Laotse and lives the life of the famous recluses, who associates himself with disgruntled persons and establishes a group for mutual admiration which declares to the world, 'A sage has arrived!' His cunning and his dark scheming mind lead him toward strange ways." Such a person could deceive the most discerning ruler and be a great danger to the state if he should ever come into power. "It is natural for a man to want to wash his face when it is dirty and to send his filthy garments to the laundry. Not so with this man! He wears a barbarian's robe and eats the food of pigs and dogs and discusses poetry and history with a convict's unshaved head and unwashed face. Now is this natural? A man who does not act according to common human nature must be a great hypocrite and a scheming intriguer." Su Hsün hoped that his prophecy was wrong, that he could be like a good general who defeats an enemy before the battle. But, he said, "if my prophecy goes wrong, people will think that these words are exaggerated and the man himself will complain of his fate. Nobody then will be aware of the calamity he could have brought upon the nation. But if these words come true, the country will be plunged into a dire calamity, and I shall be honored as a wise prophet—a sad consolation indeed!"

Whether Wang's strange habits were an affectation or not it is impossible to decide; but when a person overdoes a thing, people are inclined to suspect there is an element of conscious self-advertisement in it. If we may believe Shao Powen, Emperor Jentsung had the same suspicion. One day, at an imperial dinner given for the ministers, the guests were to catch their own fish for dinner from a pond. Before the dinner, fish bait, in the form of little pills, was laid out on gold plates on the table. Wang was not interested in fishing and began to eat the fish bait from the table and finished the plate. The next day, the Emperor said to the prime minister, "Wang Anshih is a fake. A person may well eat one pill by mistake, but no one will in a state of absent-mindedness finish them all." According to the story, that was the reason why Jentsung never liked Wang. In Wang's private diaries, he was also particularly hard against Jentsung.

In view of later developments, Su Hsün was right. Somehow in all countries, cranks and crackpots and schizophrenics have always believed that slovenliness is the mark of genius and that the best assurance of immortality is the refusal to dress like a gentleman. There is also a curious notion that filth and squalor imply contempt for material surroundings and therefore high spirituality, the logical conclusion of which is that heaven must reek with stinking angels.

When this essay was written, Su Tungp'o said that both he and his brother thought the condemnation too extreme. Only Chang Fangp'ing heartily approved. However, very soon Su Tungp'o's contemporaries were to find out how true the prediction was; and the essay survives to this day, revealing the uncanny insight of the old father.[1]

Very soon after he assumed office on the board of finance, Wang Anshih tried to test the political ground under him. Emperor Jentsung was ruling at this time, and Wang submitted to him a long memorial on governmental policies, running to about ten thousand words. In this document he enunciated the basic principles of his financial reform, the principles of "using the nation's power to produce the nation's wealth, and using the nation's wealth to provide for the nation's expenditure." He said that since the beginning of the dynasty, the government had suffered from insufficient revenue, and this resulted from the lack of a good financial and economic policy. Such a policy had not been thought of only because there were no men great enough to deal with the problems. The men in power at the time, he said, were not "great" enough for this job, nor did he think that there were other talents in the country who could be called into power. He cleverly pointed out that in making radical reforms, one should connect them with the practices of the ancient kings so that people would not regard them as a radical departure from the past. But then, he said, in following the tradition of the past, one should not copy the methods of the ancient kings, but rather their intentions, which were, after all, only for the good of the people, no matter how the policies differed. On the whole, it was a very well-written and well-organized treatise on political reforms, covering every aspect of government, including finance, civil service, and even education.

If Wang Anshih wanted to test his political ground, he found that the ground yielded under his feet. After reading the long memorandum, Emperor Jentsung laid it aside and let it sleep. During the short four-year reign of the following emperor, Yingtsung, Wang was once recalled, but again he declined office. Historians usually give the reason that he felt uneasy because he had advised against the nomination of

[1] Incorporated in a tomb inscription of Su Hsün, written by Chang Fangp'ing. Some scholars who wish to defend Wang Anshih try very hard to prove that this piece was a forgery, by pointing out that it was not included in Su Hsün's works. Su Tungp'o's own testimony, however, confirmed its genuineness.

Yingtsung as successor to Jentsung, who had died without an heir.

Meanwhile, Yingtsung's son, who was to succeed him, was living at the capital as crown prince; he later became the emperor Shentsung, under whose regime Wang Anshih came to power. While he was the crown prince, Han Wei, a great admirer of Wang Anshih, was his secretary. Han would express certain views on government, and whenever the Crown Prince liked them, he would say, "This is not my own opinion, but that of Wang Anshih." The Crown Prince, therefore, developed a very high opinion of Wang, and hoped one day he would be able to utilize his great political talents. In 1067, as soon as he ascended the throne at the age of twenty, he had Wang appointed chief magistrate of Nanking, and in September again promoted him, to the rank of a *hanlin* scholar. Wang was in constant communication with his friend and was convinced that now his opportunity had come. Contrary to his previous practice, he accepted the post at once. But he delayed coming to the capital for seven months.

"This Anshih has always declined an appointment and refused to come to the capital in the previous reigns," said Emperor Shentsung. "Some people thought he was impudent, and now again he does not come, giving illness as his excuse. Is he really ill, or is he fishing for a better post?"

At this time there was great jealousy between two veteran officials, Tseng Kungliang and Han Ch'i. The latter had served successively as premier and privy councilor under three emperors and was becoming too powerful. In his endeavor to shake Han Ch'i's position, Tseng Kungliang hoped to find in the person of Wang Anshih a powerful ally for himself. He assured the Emperor that Wang had the true caliber of a prime minister and that His Majesty should believe in him. On the other hand, another high official, Wu K'uei, who had known Wang Anshih intimately, warned the Emperor that if Wang should ever be given power he would plunge the whole country into chaos.

Finally, in April 1068, Wang Anshih, having been assured of the Emperor's attitude, appeared at the capital and was ordered to go into imperial audience with special permission to "speak out of rank"; i.e., without observance of protocol.

"What is the most important thing to do in a government?" asked the Emperor.

"To choose the right policy," answered Wang.

"What do you think of Emperor T'aitsung of Tang?" asked the Emperor again, referring to the most beloved emperor of that dynasty.

"Your Majesty should take the emperors Yao and Shun, and not merely Tang T'aitsung as your standard. The principles of Yao and Shun are really very easy to put into practice. Because the scholars of the latter days do not really understand them, they think that the standards of such a government are unattainable." (Yao and Shun were the emperors idealized by Confucius, ruling China in the semi-legendary era of the twenty-third and twenty-second centuries B.C.)

The Emperor said with some satisfaction, but modestly, "You are expecting too much of me. I am afraid I cannot live up to your high expectations."

But then there came a time for Wang Anshih to have a private audience with the Emperor alone, when the other officials had been dismissed. Here was a great chance for Wang Anshih.

"Sit down," said the Emperor. "I want to have a long talk with you." His Majesty then began to ask him why two famous emperors, one of them Tang T'aitsung, had to secure two famous scholars as their premiers to run the government. One of the two premiers mentioned was none other than Chuko Liang, probably the most renowned and capable administrator in history. Again Wang Anshih brought the discussion around to the topic of the legendary emperors of three thousand years ago.

Wang said that he preferred to talk of the able assistants of the emperors Yao and Shun. "Chuko Liang is not worth talking about in the opinion of the best minds." Chuko Liang's political genius consisted in proceeding step by step toward a definite goal, which hardly suited the impatient, self-confident wizard of finance.

"Your Majesty," continued Wang, "is now reigning over a vast empire with a huge population. After a century of peace, with so many scholars all over the land, is it not strange that no worthy men have arisen to assist Your Majesty in the government? The reason must be that Your Majesty has no decided policy and has not shown confidence in men. Though there may be great talents living at present, like those who assisted Emperors Yao and Shun, they will soon lay down their office because of obstruction by petty politicians."

"There are petty politicians in every regime," said the Emperor. "Even in the reigns of Yao and Shun there were the famous Four Evil Monsters."

"Exactly," Wang agreed. "It was because the Emperors Yao and Shun knew the four wicked ministers for what they were and had them killed that they were then able to accomplish what they did. If the four evil ministers had remained at court to carry on their machinations and intrigues, the good and able ministers would have left, too."

Shentsung, the "Divine Emperor," was duly impressed. He was only twenty, and like all young men was very ambitious and wanted to make his country strong and prosperous. He was a good and just man and he had a round and well-proportioned face, like those of his imperial ancestors. It was not until after Shentsung that the emperors of the Sung dynasty began to show distinctly degenerate traits in their physiognomy. His young enthusiasm was fired by the high expectations that Wang Anshih had entertained of him, and from that conversation on, the young emperor was ready to go through fire and water to carry through this man's political doctrines, even if it cost him all the other ministers—which

was what happened. Somehow images of the "Four Evil Monsters" appeared in the young emperor's mind whenever the wise old ministers offered counsel and advised caution against Wang Anshih's proposed reforms.

In February 1069, when the Su brothers arrived at the capital, Wang Anshih was appointed a vice-premier. The next two years were to see an exodus of all the old ministers from the court, the purging of the imperial censorate and the packing of it with Wang Anshih's own underlings. No sooner had Wang assumed office than he began to sweep the whole governmental household with a wide new broom. Protest followed protest and the whole officialdom was thrown into a deep turmoil. There was great and outspoken opposition from all ministers of proved ability and respected character. The young emperor could not understand it. Wang Anshih managed, however, to make him see the turmoil and the uproar in the light of a desperate struggle between the Emperor himself and the wicked ministers who dared to oppose his will.

"Why all this hubbub?" asked the Emperor. "Why is it that all the great ministers, censors, and scholars of the court are lined up against the new reforms?"

"You should understand," said Wang Anshih, "that Your Majesty is trying to follow the great teachings of the ancient emperors, but in order to do this you have to overcome the reactionaries. It is inevitable, therefore, that there will be a struggle for power between Your Majesty and the reactionaries. If they win in the struggle, the government will be in their hands, and if Your Majesty wins, then the power of the government will rest in the hands of Your Majesty. These selfish men are trying to obstruct the will of Your Majesty in carrying out the great teachings of the ancient emperors. That is why there is all this hubbub."

Given the earnest desire of an ambitious young ruler to make his country powerful and strong, and a premier who had an

overweening confidence in his own political
and financial theories, the stage was set for
launching the radical reforms of Wang
Anshih. The motives of such reforms cannot be questioned. It is perfectly true that
the Sung dynasty, coming after fifty years
of disunity and internecine strife, had never
known a strong government. Besides, the
Hsi Hsias, the Khitans (later called the
Liaos), and the Chins had been making
constant inroads into China's northern border. Brief wars with these northern tribes
were followed by temporary treaties of uneasy peace. The terms of the treaties were
humiliating to a Chinese emperor, for while
some of these kingdoms acknowledged the
emperor, it was not they but the emperor
who had to give annual contributions in
silver and silks to the northern tribes, running anywhere from a hundred thousand
to a quarter of a million dollars a year. This
acted as a tremendous drain on the imperial
treasury. The domestic administration had
always been lax, and the government was
constantly running into financial deficits.
Wang Anshih believed that he was a great
financial wizard who could raise money for
the imperial treasury by juggling with the
systems of taxation and conscription. I believe that the desire to build China into a
powerful state and to increase the prestige
of the empire through wars of conquest in
the northwest were prime factors in influ-
encing the young Emperor Shentsung in
Wang Anshih's favor, for Wang's administration was characterized by several wars
started by China with the northern tribes,
some victories and one disastrous defeat.
In order to carry on wars, the Emperor
needed money, and in order to have money,
the country's financial system had to be
reorganized. Yet, without ever questioning
the sincere motives of the reformer, we shall
see how these reforms, financial and economic in character, produced the most
grievous consequences of a different nature.

Soon after Wang Anshih had arrived at
the capital, Ssu-ma Kuang had an argument
with him in the Emperor's presence which
seems to sum up the fundamental opposition of the two sides. The imperial treasury
was actually impoverished at this time, and
during an important ceremony at the wor-
ship of Heaven in spring, the Emperor
wished to dispense with the customary gifts
of silver and silks to the officials, thus saving
some money for the imperial household.
This started an argument between Ssu-ma
Kuang and Wang Anshih. Wang Anshih
maintained that the national treasury was
impoverished only because the officials did
not understand finance.

"What you mean by finance," countered
Ssu-ma Kuang, "is only increase of taxation
and levies from the people."

"No," said Wang Anshih. "A good finan-
cier can increase the government revenue
without increasing taxation."

"What nonsense! After all, a nation pos-
sesses a definite amount of wealth, and this
wealth is either in the hands of the people
or in those of the government. No matter
what measures you carry out or by what
names you call them, they can only mean
taking away part of the wealth of the people and giving it to the government."

The Emperor was inclined to agree with
Ssu-ma Kuang, and for a month or two the
measures were held in abeyance.

Without being an economist, one is safe
to accept the general thesis that the two
factors in a nation's wealth are production
and distribution. To increase a nation's
wealth, one must increase its productivity
or have a better distribution of goods. In
Wang Anshih's day, however, increase of
production was out of the question, since
there was no means of industrialization.
Therefore, all that a financial wizard could
do would be in the line of distribution.
Since Wang was primarily interested in
enriching the national treasury, increase of
the nation's wealth strictly meant the increase of the government's revenue. Wang
saw clearly that the rich merchants and
landlords were making money in a system
of free enterprise, and he could not see
why the government should not take away
the profits from free enterprise and run

business and make the money itself. The conclusion was inevitable. The terms he used were actually strikingly modern. He wanted to stop "monopoly" (*chienping*) by capital; he wanted to equalize wealth by "taking it away from the rich and giving it to the poor"; he wanted to prevent the peasants from borrowing from landlords at high interest. It would be a great and charitable measure on the part of the government to lend money to the peasants during spring planting and have them return the money when the crops were harvested. Wang Anshih was able to convince the Emperor that all these measures were "for the good of the people"; but history records that after a period of hesitancy, the thing that decided him on launching the loans was the argument of a certain minor official that with an investment of half a million dollars, the government stood to earn a quarter of a million dollars in interest per year, since there were two crops and the twenty or thirty per cent interest could be collected twice a year.

Without going too much into the details of the various reforms, which were started in 1069 and ended disastrously about eight years later when both Wang Anshih himself and the Emperor were thoroughly sick of them and of each other, we may give a brief summary of these measures.

The most important and the best known were nine in number, which I have for the sake of convenience arranged in three groups. There were three state capitalist enterprises, three new taxes, and three systems of registration for a complete regimentation and control of the people. The three state capitalist enterprises were: a government bureau for national trade, a bureau for government stores in retail trade, and the famous loans to the farmers with an official interest of twenty per cent and an actual interest of thirty per cent (i.e., plus application and registration charges). The three new taxes were the draft exemption tax, the excise tax, and the income tax. The systems of registration were the organizing of all citizens into groups of ten

families for military draft (the *paochia*), and the re-registration of land and of horses. In general, all these measures suggest the tendency to economic collectivism of modern days.

The state capitalist enterprises began in July 1069 with the establishing of a bureau for national or interprovincial wholesale trade. Convinced of the great profits to accrue to the government, the Emperor allocated a sum of five million dollars in cash and thirty million bushels of rice as capital with which the government would take over the interprovincial trade in goods and raw materials. Immediately this system ran into practical difficulties. In February of the same year a bureau of economic planning was established, charged with the duty of studying the plans and programs before promulgation. Among the staff of the planning bureau was Su Tungp'o's brother, Tseyu. In his memorandum Tseyu pointed out that when the government took over the national trade, free enterprise would at once be paralyzed, for local dealers would be handicapped in competition with the government. It was inevitable that the government and the businessmen would be treading on each other's toes. Moreover, he denied that the imperial treasury stood to gain. While private business worked through an established system of credits and other arrangements, the government lacked these facilities. It must first set up a big staff with high salaries and beautiful office buildings. It would not be doing business according to supply and demand but instead would make transactions on the merit of commissions, distributing favors and contracts according to personal connections. Tseyu argued that, short of forcing down the price of its purchases by official pressure, through sheer bureaucratic incompetence the government would buy at a higher price than independent businessmen were able to get. Therefore it stood to lose.

This so-called government wholesale trade was, therefore, stopped for a year's further study; then the government came out with a modified program under a new name. The division between wholesale and retail was not a hard and fast one, and trade bureaus in charge of the large government-run stores were established in big cities such as Chengtu, Canton, and Hangchow. Another government grant of a million dollars from the national treasury and $870,000 in the local currency of the capital was allocated for the development of these trade bureaus. The reasons advanced for their establishment were that "the country's goods had fallen into the hands of capital monopolists" and that "the prices of goods fluctuated from time to time because of capitalist manipulations; in order to rule the country peacefully, one should take away the wealth from the rich and give it to the poor." A very capable official was put at the head, and the more profits he was able to report to the government, the more capable he was considered to be. This Lu Chiawen became a kind of trade dictator of the country, having monopoly control of the small businessmen. The rules of the trade bureau at the capital, for instance, were that the small traders were to become affiliated members of the bureau; that these small traders could pool their goods with the bureau's assets, or that the government would provide the capital for purchasing stocks for the stores run by them; that in case traders wished to liquidate their business and hand over the goods to the government bureau they would be permitted to do so; that they could use part of their goods as security for cash advances from the government for which they were to pay an interest of ten per cent per half year or twenty per cent a year; that others not connected with the bureau would also be permitted to sell their stocks to it at prices fixed by the government; and that, finally, all imperial purchases, by whatever department, would be transacted through the trade bureau.

The government's absorption of small business was one of the worst features of the regime, and private business came almost to a standstill. In a few years trade and commerce actually decreased so that the government revenue was affected to an alarming degree, in spite of the theoretical high profits. The Emperor found himself, to his great disgust, degenerating in the eyes of the people into a petty peddler selling fruits, ice and coal, calendars, and straw mats. In the end it was the scandal connected with the trade bureau at the capital and the excise tax that reached the ears of the imperial household and caused the Emperor to put a stop to the most unpopular features of the reform.

But the most widely known of the new reforms in this regime was the farmers' loans, and to this day when people speak of Wang Anshih's reforms they always think first of these loans. It was a measure that affected every village of the empire and precipitated the biggest political battle among the ministers at the court. In itself the plan was good and sound, suggesting the idea of a farmers' bank. While serving as a young magistrate, Wang Anshih had made loans to the farmers during spring planting and collected them with interest when the harvest was in. He had found that this was a real help to the farmers because in a local administration he could see to it that the farmers came to borrow money only in actual cases of need, and upon proper personal investigation. In Shensi the local authorities also tried this scheme with success, and it was from the practice started in Shensi that the farmers' loans received their Chinese name of "seedling loans."

In a good year, when the authorities were sure of good crops, they made loans to enable the farmers to purchase equipment and seedlings for their wheat fields; and when the harvest came, they were able to collect grains for the army with an advantageous interest. In the words of the bureau of economic planning, "It is proposed that the money and grain from the price equalization granaries be loaned to people upon application, following the example of Shensi province. They may be asked to pay an interest of twenty per cent, which they will pay together with the capital during the collection of the summer and autumn taxes. People who wish to repay the loans in cash in place of grain may be permitted to do so. In case of natural calamities, they may be permitted to delay the repayment until a good year comes. Thus not only will the people be able to tide over famine and drought, but through these loans they will be spared the necessity of borrowing from the rich exploiters at double interest before their harvest is in. Besides, the stocks of wheat and grain are now usually kept in the price equalization granaries for a long time and sold to the people only when the prices have gone up, and this system benefits only the idle rich who live in the cities. It is proposed now that such sales and purchases be organized and unified within each province, so that price stabilization may be better carried out and the farmers enabled to plant their farms without being exploited. All this is for the benefit of the people and without profits to the government. It is in accordance with the principles of the ancient kings in giving money to the people and assisting the farmers."

How such a beautiful and innocent plan turned out to harass and destroy the lives and homes of the farmers for whose benefit it was conceived, we shall see later. It should be explained, however, that this new measure started as a continuation of the old system of the price equalization granaries and gradually replaced it. From the very beginning of this dynasty, such granaries had been maintained in different districts by the government to stabilize the price of grains. In years of good crops, when low prices hit the farmers hard, the government bought up the surplus wheat and rice. Conversely, in bad years, when the prices of grain went up, the agencies poured the grain into the market to force the prices down. It is true that the agencies were not always kept up to their highest efficiency, for many officials did not bother to buy up grain when it was cheap. But even in 1066 the published figures of the price equalization granaries showed that

they had bought from the people 5,014,180 bushels of grain and sold 4,711,570 bushels during that year. Now, when the money and stocks of the granaries were used as capital for the farmers' loans, the normal operations of the granaries were naturally stopped.

The heart of the matter was that the subscription of the loans inevitably became compulsory. Intolerant of opposition, Wang Anshih had to succeed. He had to show the Emperor that the loans were a great success and were welcomed by the people. He would not hear of slackness in selling them. He could not understand why the farmers should not want the loans, and when loans were not sold up to the quota, he flew into a rage. He began to promote officials who showed a good record, and to punish the slackers. As each official was looking out for his own career, his most important concern was to make a good report. The incentive for personal competition was very much like the selling of government bonds in modern days. When the officials knew that they would be cashiered and degraded for "blocking reforms" if they did not sell up to their quota, it was inevitable that loans began to be allocated by official pressure, by what Wang was pleased to call the "energetic" officials. Every family had to borrow from the government, and everybody had to pay thirty per cent interest for a period of three months. There were good officials who knew what harm these loans were causing the poor people and the certainty of their being put in jail for failure to repay capital and interest. These took the government at its word and announced to the public that these loans, according to the imperial decree, were strictly "voluntary"; and they were prepared to be degraded for "blocking reforms" when the day of reckoning came.

In the draft exemption tax also, there was a great discrepancy between official intentions and actual practice. This was probably the best reform put through by Wang Anshih, and it was this measure which Su Tungp'o alone defended against his own party, when the latter was in power and was determined to wipe out each and every one of Wang Anshih's reforms.

For a long time the people of China had been subjected to conscription for military service. The proposal was that the people should pay a tax in place of the conscription. In other words, it meant replacing a military draft system by a standing army of hired and paid soldiers. However, from a careful study of the rules of this draft exemption, one cannot escape the conclusion that the government was primarily interested in the revenue from the tax, and whatever benefit it had in relieving the people from military draft was nullified entirely by the *paochia* system which was even worse as a form of compulsory draft. After careful deliberation for over a year, the regulations were published. They provided that families which had been exempt from the military draft were also compelled to pay the draft exemption tax; for example, widows, families without children or with only one son or with children not of age, and nuns and monks, were compelled to pay the tax under a different name, called "the draft-aid tax." Moreover, twenty per cent was added to the regular tax over and above district draft quotas, nominally to provide against the bad years when the people might not be able to pay. With the money collected from this tax, soldiers and other employees of the government were to be hired. Just as Su Tseyu had pointed out in the case of the farmers' loans that the people would be put in prison and whipped for default, so Ssu-ma Kuang pointed out now exactly what happened later, that people who had no cash to pay this tax in autumn and summer—when all the other taxes came—would be compelled to sell their grain, kill their cows, and cut down trees in order to obtain the cash. Moreover, in the preceding system of military draft, the people took turns serving for a period of years, whereas in the new system the people were compelled to pay for exemption every year, including the years when they would not have to serve.

Together with the new excise tax and the income tax, this draft exemption tax must be viewed principally as a new means to raise revenue from the people, rather than to relieve them of the draft for service, since the people were drafted for military training under another name, the *paochia*. The excise tax was a tax on the profits of businessmen, based on an examination of their books. The income tax was not an income tax in the modern sense. I call it income tax here because it was a system of compulsory registration of a citizen's income and property as a basis for allocation of the other taxes. It was like the income tax also in the sense that the people had to make returns of their income and property, under pain of defrauding the government. In the fight over this reform it was stated that after the order was issued, there was "not a chicken or a pig on a farm, or an inch of soil, or a beam or rafter in a roof" that was not reported and registered with the government. This last measure, instituted in 1074, was short-lived because Wang soon went out of power; and even before its suspension Su Tungp'o refused to enforce it in the district under his control on the ground that it was illegal.

What gave the lie to Wang Anshih's desire to relieve the people from military draft, professed in the preceding draft exemption tax, was the *paochia* system. This is clear because both the new *paochia* system and the draft exemption tax were promulgated in the same month, December 1070. The government took away the burden of military service from the people with one hand by making them pay for the "exemption," and put it back on the people with the other. The *paochia* was a system for collective guarantee under the law of families living in the same neighborhood. Each ten families were organized into a *pao*, and each fifty families formed a great *pao*. The members of a *pao* were to be collectively responsible in cases of harboring criminals and thieves; and in cases of such crimes as murder and rape they were bound to report the circumstances to the court. Able-bodied persons in each great *pao* were to be organized into a company for military drill and training, a family with two able-bodied males contributing one, and a family of more than two males contributing more in proportion. These were to leave their farms for drill every fifth day, the five-day period being the ancient equivalent of the week, dividing a month conveniently into six periods. Thus instead of taking the sons of the families to the army as in the regular draft system, this reform brought the army right into the village. But Wang Anshih was a great propagandist; he knew that by giving a thing a new name, he made it cease to exist. "Conscription was abolished."

Besides this collective registration and regimentation of the people, there was also a new and compulsory registration of the farmers' lands as a basis for the new taxes, and a system of farming out the government's cavalry to be cared for by the farmers. Like all other collectivistic systems, Wang Anshih's administration could not leave the people alone. In its anxiety to take good care of them, the government had to know exactly what the people did and what they possessed. Like all other collectivistic systems also, this regime found it impossible to govern without secret agents, which were instituted in the year 1072, luckily after Su Tungp'o had left the capital. Nor was it able to operate without bringing under control the imperial censorate, the equivalent of the modern press, and packing it with the party's underlings who were willing to follow strictly the party line. Again, Wang Anshih considered it necessary to control the thoughts and ideas of the scholars. Like Wang Mang of the ancient days, and like the modern Hitler, he had the idea of one state, one belief, and one leader. Like Hitler, he exploded in fits of temper when he encountered opposition; modern psychiatrists might classify him as a paranoiac.

What showed the "paranoid" character of the man, and what all historians and critics agree to have been his one in-

excusable act, was not any of his political or socialistic ventures, but his setting up himself now as the one and only interpreter of the classics. As Wang Mang re-edited and falsified the ancient classics, so now Wang Anshih wrote his own interpretation of three Confucian classics and made it the official guide to thinking, to replace all the great commentators of the past. Wang was a fairly good scholar, but not good enough to replace the great masters of the past, such as Cheng Hsüan, Ma Yung, Lu Tehming, and others. To do this was both an abuse of his official power and an insult to scholarship. The examination papers were usually upon passages from the classics, and candidates' interpretations had to conform. Setting up this new standard, therefore, meant that every scholar of the land had to study and absorb what Wang Anshih said on every topic, from principles of government and Buddhist-colored Confucianism to the etymology for "quail," "owl," and "pheasant." After leaving the capital, Su Tungp'o had once to supervise a local examination, and wrote a poem recording his disgust with the deadening uniformity of thought and ideas expressed by the candidates in the papers.

Like his philology, Wang's *New Commentaries on the Three Classics,* often savoring of Buddhist ideas, showed more originality than sound scholarship. He believed, however, that in the interpretation of the ancient ideas and political systems, whatever he thought was so must therefore be so. These *Commentaries* were so bad that they were soon forgotten after his death, and no copy has been preserved. But while he was in power, they were the bible of the scholar candidates at the examinations; the slightest variation from the interpretation of the premier was enough to disqualify a paper. Particularly it showed offense to scholarship to have the compilation of the *Commentaries* made in only two years; the work was formally started in March 1073, with the help of his young son and a political henchman, and published in June 1075. This hurried piece of work was set up as the orthodox interpretation of Confucianism, and as Wang changed his mind about the interpretations, new versions were published for the benefit of the scholar candidates who knew their lives depended on keeping abreast of the revisions. . . .

Some Chinese scholars of later days, following Western ideas of collectivism, have tried to rescue Wang Anshih from historical infamy and revise his reputation upward by showing that his ideas were essentially "in conformity with modern socialism." Among those who took up the defense of Wang Anshih was a great modern scholar, Liang Ch'ich'ao. It would be possible to argue the pros and cons of Wang's socialistic ideas, but Wang's socialistic regime must be judged by its results. The facts are that in place of "private monopoly" the state set up its own monopoly; small businessmen were thrown out of jobs, and farmers, unable to repay the compulsory loans or keep up the interest, sold their wives and children or fled, and their neighbors who were made guarantors of the loans fled with them or sold or mortgaged their properties. The country jails were full, every district government found thousands of closed mortgages and confiscated properties on its hands, and lawsuits filled the courts. It was a misrule that would have ruined any dynasty, even if there were no foreign invaders. In 1074 an imperial edict said that business was at a standstill and people were thrown out of their jobs; and another edict in 1076, which stopped the loans, said that many were jailed and flogged for failure to repay them. In a memorandum sent in June 1090, some twenty years later, when he was trying to salvage the economic wreckage left of the countryside and begging for restoration of confiscated properties and forgiveness of all debts of the poor, Su Tungp'o wrote:

Since the order to return the confiscated properties, the people are overjoyed. They have said to me that since they were driven out from their homes and business, parents have been separated from their children and wives from their husbands, living the life of homeless, wandering refugees. Since the establishment of the trade bureaus and government stores, all means of livelihood of the people have been taken over by the government. The small traders, deprived of their normal trade, were forced to join up with the government trade bureaus and compelled to mortgage their goods and properties to obtain immediate cash at a high interest. When the loans matured and they were not able to repay, they were fined double interest. Gradually their debts piled higher and higher, and more and more people were put in jail together with their families.

For the first few years, however, Wang Anshih was able to keep the Emperor in the dark about the terrible conditions by adroit propaganda, insisting he had the "people's support" for his "agrarian program" and painting a totalitarian regime as a "democracy"—a confusion of terms strangely reminiscent of modern days. Then as now, whether a people love a regime or not can be judged only when a despotic regime is no longer in power. Sincere in his desire to learn the truth, the Emperor sent out his own reporters. But knowing that the reforms were popular with the Emperor himself, the eunuchs and dishonest reporters always reported to the Emperor that the people loved the reforms, and that upon the arrival of the tax commissioners, the "people cried with joy," which was literally true, as far as a staged reception was concerned. The terrible conditions of the people after a few years of Wang Anshih's regime were at last revealed to the Emperor in the form of pictures submitted by a curious, obscure palace gatekeeper, a very daring man.

Standing at the gate, this official, Cheng Hsia, saw the hordes of refugees who had fled from the northeast and were swarming the streets of the capital. Knowing that pictures spoke louder than words, Cheng Hsia conceived the idea of making pictures of these poor farmers and presenting them to the Emperor. Here was a picture of the refugees, half clad and starving, traveling on the highway in a blinding storm. There was a picture of half-naked men and women eating grass roots and tree bark, and others working in chains carrying bricks and firewood to sell to pay the taxes. Upon seeing the pictures, the Emperor shed tears. It was this dramatic presentation, which we shall come to later, coupled with the appearance of a spectacular comet and a landslide on a sacred mountain, that made the Emperor suspend many of the "reforms.". . .

The tragedy of Wang Anshih comes from the fact that he was not in any way self-indulgent or corrupt himself, and that his hand was forced. To carry out anything so radical as his state capitalist program, he knew he had to override all opposition. Perhaps that was why he had bided his time so long. He had a vision, and his wagon was hitched to that starry vision, not of a happy, peaceful and prosperous nation, but of a rich, strong, and powerful state, expanding its borders north and south. God had willed that the Sung dynasty was to be great and expansionist, like the Hans and the Tangs, and he, Wang Anshih, was the manifest Man of Destiny. But there is not one "Man of Destiny" who does not appear slightly pathetic in the contemplation of future historians—a man caught in the prison of his ambition, a victim of his own dream, which grew and expanded and then burst like a bubble.

Despising all the "conservative philistines," he not only alienated the good old ministers but even lost Han Wei and Lü Kungchu who were his best friends. Han Wei, we remember, was the friend who had turned Shentsung's heart and hopes toward Wang Anshih when the former was crown prince. When these friends disagreed with him on the manner in which he carried out his projects, he had no hesitation in banishing them from the court. Deserted and alone, he took in and promoted unknown and unqualified men who were smart enough to agree with him and use him for their own purposes. To make it easier to distinguish the three notorious

characters, I have given them a more familiar spelling: Leeding, Sudan, and Dunquan. Leeding was a man who concealed the news of his mother's death to avoid going out of office, a daring offense in Confucian society. Dunquan is remembered by posterity as the author of the famous saying, "Let them all laugh who want to laugh; a good official post is mine." But the arch supporters of Wang Anshih were two extremely active and persuasive talkers of great scheming ability, Tseng Pu and Lü Huich'ing, particularly the latter, who eventually double-crossed Wang Anshih in an effort to supersede him. The collapse of this eight-year regime was summarized by a contemporary as follows: "Huich'ing sold out Wang Anshih, Wang Anshih sold out the Emperor, and the Emperor sold out the people." When Huich'ing stooped to publishing Wang's private letters to alienate him from the Emperor, Wang was overthrown, and in his old age he used to spend his fury over the turncoat friend by scribbling the word "Fukienite" a few times every day, Fukien being the province from which Huich'ing came. When Su Tungp'o met Wang Anshih in Nanking after the regime was over, and rebuked him for starting wars and persecuting scholars, Wang replied that Huich'ing was responsible for all the doings. This is hardly a plausible defense, since it was Wang himself who insisted on dealing harshly with all opposition, and since the institution of espionage at the capital against critics of the government was established during the period when Huich'ing was in retirement in mourning for his father, between April 1071 and July 1073.

Otherwise, the two leaders of the opposite factions, Wang Anshih and Ssu-ma Kuang, while uncompromising in their fight over government policies, were both sincere in their convictions and above reproach in their private lives. Neither was ever accused of corruption in money matters or of looseness of morals, while Ouyang Hsiu was at least alleged to have had some affairs in his private household.

Once Wang Anshih's wife, Wu, had bought a concubine for her husband. When the woman was presented, Wang asked, in surprise, "What is that thing?"

"The Madame has asked me to serve you," replied the woman.

"But who are you?" asked Wang again.

"My husband," replied the woman, "was working with the army in charge of a boatload of government rice. The boat sank and he lost the whole cargo. We sold all our property to restore the loss but still could not make up the amount. And so my husband sold me to pay for the balance."

"How much were you sold for?" asked Wang.

"Nine hundred dollars."

Wang Anshih sent for her husband and bade the woman go back to him, telling him to keep the money.

The same thing happened to Ssu-ma Kuang, for he, too, had a concubine against his wish. In his younger days he was serving as a deputy magistrate and his wife had not yet produced a son for him. The chief magistrate's wife presented him with a concubine, but Ssu-ma Kuang ignored her. Thinking that it was because of her own presence, his wife one day asked the girl to wait till she was out of the house and then dress up and go into his study at night. When Ssu-ma Kuang saw the girl appear in his room, he said in surprise to the girl, "How dare you come here? The Madame is away," and he sent her away. Both men were more interested in carrying out their policies than in personal power, and Wang Anshih certainly had no regard for money. While he was premier, as soon as his salary was received, he turned it over to his brothers to spend it any way they liked.

Ssu-ma Kuang, who towered intellectually and morally above his generation, fought a clean-cut battle of principles from the beginning to the end. He and Wang Anshih stood at opposite poles on government policy. In the words of a contemporary, "Wang Anshih refused to be premier unless the new policies were carried out, and Ssu-ma Kuang refused to be vice privy councilor unless the new policies were abolished."

The Historical Task Facing Wang An-shih and the Road of Reformism He Took

TENG KUANG-MING

Appraisal of Wang An-shih from the viewpoint of Chinese Communism seems to be moving ahead rather slowly. The present selection is from a biography of Wang by Teng Kuang-ming (1910–   ), who was a member of the Faculty of History in Peking University when he wrote the book. Although not one of the best-known scholars of China and apparently not a member of the Communist Party, Teng has done other studies in the Sung period, such as a biography of the Southern Sung general Yo Fei, work on the poet Hsin Ch'i-chi, and a commentary on Sung officials published in the *Bulletin* of the Institute of History and Philology of Academia Sinica in 1948. His essay may therefore suggest the approach to Wang that may be expected from scholars in the Chinese People's Republic. That more will be heard about Wang from that quarter is indicated in the appearance of an article in *Lishi Yanjiu* 10 (1958) by Hou Wai-lu and Chu Han-sheng, entitled, "Wang An-shih, A Materialist Philosopher in the Sung Dynasty."

THE Sung house had seized political power by dark and crafty means. Because they sought the protection and support of the powerful gentry and landlord class, the Sung government not only could not restrict the evil of oppressive concentrations of landholdings but used its political power to protect and abet powerful gentry and landlords. Accompanying the adoption of policies of this kind, there came a great continual increase of the numbers of peasants who lost their land and continually a deeper hatred and more intense struggle by the exploited workers against the exploiting classes.

The Ch'i-tan tribes of the northern borders, since the founding of their state [Liao] in the early years of the tenth century, had grown ever more powerful, and when in 936 Shih Ching-t'ang [founder of the Later Chin dynasty, r. 936–943] ceded the Sixteen Prefectures of Yen and Yün [a section of territory along the northern borders of Hopei and Shansi] to them, Ch'i-tan strength reached its height. From the day when the Sung state was founded, the broad region it held from the Yellow River north had been constantly under the threat of this strong neighbor. In the closing years of the tenth century, the power of the Tangut tribes also developed, and because of this Sung could not feel secure on its northwest borders either.

From this it can be seen that from the founding of Sung political power, two great questions facing the state had been how to resolve this severe class struggle and how to remove the threat against national security raised by the strong Ch'i-tan tribes.

From Teng Kuang-ming, *Wang An-shih*. Peking: San-lien Shu-tien, 1953. pp. 27–38. Translated by the editor of this volume.

In fact, these two questions were only two aspects of a single condition. If the Sung government could handle the peasant problem satisfactorily, it could naturally increase its power to resist the foreigners. But this is what Chao K'uang-yin [Sung T'ai-tsu], his successors, and the great ministers they had respectively employed had failed to recognize. For them, the only consideration was that the Sung government had not the strength to solve both of these great problems simultaneously. On these grounds, they decided that in regard to the clash of peoples, they must use compromise and concession to the utmost, adopting a passive policy of accommodation; they would concentrate their strength in activities to control and repress the people, hoping thus to make it impossible for the peasants to rise up; or if they should, to prevent the rebellion from spreading very far. From the military system and the disposition of military forces throughout the Sung, we can clearly see that this was the basic policy.

The Sung military system followed the enlistment system that had been begun in the middle period of T'ang. One effect of the enlistment system was that it enrolled in the ranks a good number of unemployed vagabonds, turning the strength of a group potentially opposed to the existing political authority into a force for the protection of that authority. The Sung dynasty furthered this function of the system, exploiting it to the full. Whenever the harvest was not good, it enlisted great numbers of starving people as soldiers, bringing them together under the care and direction of the ruling class and in return obliged to serve the ruling class. The numbers of troops increased sharply, from 200,000 at the beginning of Sung to 1,600,000 by about 1065.

The only reason why the Sung Court enlisted these masses of starving and rootless people was to weaken the power of the ruled class to struggle. Since the Sung Court was aware of the questionable effectiveness in battle of a rabble of enlisted soldiers, it increased the number of troops

under its control constantly, but it dared not put them to use in battle against the foreigners. Furthermore, according to the estimates of the Sung Court, the incursions of the foreigners were only a kind of warfare for plunder; they were not an imminent threat to the rule. What could at any time endanger that rule, even overturn its sovereignty, was a rebellion of the oppressed peasantry. In the light of this estimate, the Sung Court only chose a number of the most select troops to station on the borders and charged them with defense, never daring to turn their defensive capacity into an offensive one. The vast majority of troops beyond these were all stationed in the central region, especially in Kaifeng, the capital, and in districts near Kaifeng. Lü Tsu-ch'ien [historian and classicist, 1137–1181] of Southern Sung pointed out the principles of military management in the Northern Sung dynasty: "To police the land in times of peace, to garrison strategic places, to abandon territory to the enemy, to guard against what was within and ignore what was without, to regard the normal function of an army [combat against a foreign enemy] as to be used only in emergency, and to look upon what should be easy [victory over smaller forces] as difficult." The reason for this was entirely to prevent "popular insurrections."

The results of this management of military affairs were not at all what the Sung Court expected. To the contrary, they created a number of problems, as follows: (1) As a result of adopting a consistently weak and compromising policy against the foreigners, [the Sung] exposed its own military impotence and correspondingly emboldened the spirit of Liao (the Ch'i-tan) and Hsi Hsia (the Tangut). By the middle of the eleventh century, these two countries had formed a two-pronged threat, the Hsi Hsia regularly mounting attacks and Liao regularly taking advantage of them to demand concessions. (2) The military weakness which was exposed in war and the repeated defeats the Sung Court suffered wiped out its military prestige, inevitably weakening its effectiveness in holding the people down. (3) Farmers who had lost their land and been enlisted limitlessly in the ranks, coming under the care of the government, could not return to their productive rounds. This necessarily exerted a severe influence on agriculture, resulting in the evil of diminished production. (4) The numbers of troops increasing constantly, the cost of maintaining them increased correspondingly. The Sung Court adopted all the methods of oppressing the people that had been used in past history and stretched and raised the oppressive aspects to the limit. From the fortieth year of the eleventh century on, the Sung Court used eighty per cent and more of financial revenues obtained by these methods for maintaining the troops. The people were stripped clean of their flesh, but still the government's finances seemed constantly inadequate. (5) The result of enlisting large numbers of dispossessed peasants in the army and of increasing limitlessly the tax burden on the masses of the people was to create continually more unemployed. Since the Sung Court could not possibly enlist all of them, and they for their part did not want to be enlisted, when they assembled in a strong band they would attack towns and outposts and deal revenge to the hated ruling classes at their head. From the twentieth year of the eleventh century on, peasant risings not only grew more frequent year by year but stronger band by band. In the fortieth year of the century, in Shantung and Huainan in the east; Loyang, Ju-chou and Shan-chou in the west; Hsiang-yang and Teng-chou in the south—in all these places peasant risings occurred one after another.

When Wang An-shih received Chao Hsü's [Shen-tsung's] summons to return to Kaifeng and was appointed by him a councillor, in fact with broad authority to conduct the government, the problems noted above were all intertwined intricately in society, in its political and economic spheres, and awaited his solutions.

If we were to take the position of the most cruelly oppressed and exploited workers and peasants and seek a way of solving the problems above, it could have been only to adopt the methods of revolution: to overthrow the old political authority and impose order and improvement on the manner of land-tenure. But Wang An-shih was a man of the bureaucrat-landlord class, an element of the ruling class. Even so, because of his profundity of learning, sincerity of conduct and wealth of experience, his mind had already been somewhat broadened and his vision lengthened, so that he clearly recognized that if great reforms were not administered to government and economics, the impact of unproductive, unemployed peasants must continually increase until there would be no way to avoid a general peasant uprising. However, this was quite the farthest limit of Wang An-shih's "vision." To expect that he would disavow his own class and stand firmly with the peasant class, making his sole concern the direct producers and the poor and hired peasants; that he would walk the road that they must walk and use revolutionary means to struggle to achieve a reform of economic life— this, on the contrary, would be absolutely impossible. It would not only be impossible. In Wang An-shih's Ten Thousand Word Memorial, written to Chao Chen [Sung Jen-tsung, r. 1023–1064], he himself had early raised the rebellions of Chang Chüeh at the end of Han and Huang Ch'ao at the end of T'ang as examples to show what Chao Chen must quickly prevent. Obviously he himself was completely opposed to peasant revolutions.

Follow the past completely; change not a bit of it: Ssu-ma Kuang and others, representatives of the powerful gentry and big landlord class, were proponents of this kind of view. They only hoped to exploit political power to the full to protect the rights and privileges their own class already had and to strengthen their control over the direct producers. If the unproducing, starving people reached the point of rising up, it was only, according to the simple explanation of these men, because of a slackening of military control and insufficiently strong government repression. All that was needed to meet and solve this problem was to strengthen these two oppressive forces. To undertake political and economic reforms was completely unnecessary. Wang An-shih, even in his youth, had been dissatisfied with the abnormal political structure and economic development of the times. After long experience in government he evolved in his mind a number of concrete plans for reforming the existing government and society. The powerful gentry and big landlords were the very objects he thought it necessary to set to order. Therefore, the extremely conservative way of Ssu-ma Kuang and others was just what Wang An-shih completely opposed.

Opposed to the way of the past which the powerful gentry and big landlords would follow completely; yet also fearing the way of revolution, of overturning the existing political authority, that the bankrupt peasants, sunk to the lowest levels of life, might take: this makes it clear that Wang An-shih represented the political demands of the middle and small landlord classes. Moreover, he would pay appropriate attention to the economic rights and benefits in general of middle peasants, rich peasants, small merchants, and independent hand craftsmen. This determined the way that Wang An-shih could adopt: it could only be the way of reformism.

As has been said, Wang An-shih recognized that if the rather poor political and economic management before his eyes were accepted and continued to be administered, large numbers of middle and small landlords could not avoid losing their land and becoming rootless, and many of the well-off peasants would be pushed off their land. The result would be the outbreak of a universal and large-scale peasant rising. Wang An-shih feared the development of such an event and felt that the only way to alleviate the critical situation was for the rulers to give some concrete benefits to the great masses. This required putting into operation in both political and economic

spheres reforming activities within certain limits. Therefore, Wang An-shih's point of view was different from that of Chao Hsü, who demanded political reforms only to achieve a rich country and strong defense. The important portions of Wang's program of reform were based on the economic demands of society.

Wang An-shih advocated "full use of the human resources of the country to produce the wealth of the country." He advocated using the government's strength vigorously to aid the peasants, enabling them to work under the most favorable conditions. He advocated the government's enacting some measures of advantage to the cultivators and not of advantage to powerful monopolizing families, and gradually to correct somewhat the existing exploitive and slave labor systems. We must point out that if these principles of Wang An-shih could have been carried out in practice, objectively speaking, they would have contributed positively to the advancement of society at the time.

Since reform work must be pushed forward by government, coming from the top and going to the bottom, Wang An-shih realized that he must first capture Chao Hsü to make him support the New Laws positively enough. Since Chao Hsü knew only that he wanted a rich country and a strong defense and did not recognize the need for economic reform in society, Wang An-shih explained all the economic reforms as intimately related to enriching the country and strengthening defense. For example, Chao Hsü gave great attention to acts to "order finances," and Wang An-shih also acknowledged the importance of ordering finances. He explained to Chao Hsü, however, that in ordering finances, attending to agricultural matters was of immediate importance. And what to do about agriculture? It was necessary, in the negative aspect, to relieve the peasants of their suffering, repress the monopolists, and enable the general cultivators to breathe a bit more easily under the oppression of the powerful gentry, big landlords and moneylenders.

In the positive aspect, the peasants should be aided by river and land conservancy and by giving them timely material aid, so that they might farm diligently. By arguments like this Wang An-shih tactfully and persuasively explained things to Chao Hsü, and only after he, too, had been brought to a fairly clear comprehension did Wang go on to the reform work of the Tribute Transport and Distribution, Hired-Services and other measures.

Under the long protection of Sung political authority, the powerful gentry and big landlords completely controlled the political machinery. Public opinion also was in their grasp, they had the power of manipulating the government, and their influence on the emperors was especially great. Although in Wang An-shih's new political program there were provisions for striking at the powerful monopolists, and this was of the highest priority in order to benefit the middle and small landlords and rich peasants, the reformist Wang An-shih nevertheless did not dare to plan radically to overthrow the powerful gentry and big landlord class from its social and economic foundations.

He thought only to limit by means of laws the rights and benefits they had already obtained; and even the limitation was to be limited. He realized that if he struck at the powerful gentry and big landlords with excessive severity, that would make them rise up against the New Laws and obstruct them. They could incite townsmen to beat the drums outside magistrates' gates and demand a hearing for their grievances; they could intercept the Emperor's sedan-chair on the highway; they could besiege great ministers' offices and houses—in this way and that they could appeal that the New Laws ought not to be carried out, and so forth. This caused Wang An-shih to make compromises everywhere, and voluntarily to make rather great concessions to the powerful gentry and big landlords. This in turn caused the total results of Wang An-shih's political reforms to fall far short of the mark at which he had aimed. And because the powerful gentry and big landlords were not overthrown, the New Laws effected by Wang An-shih and the results they had already achieved ultimately fell into the hands of representatives of that class.

The Reforms of Wang An-shih

ICHISADA MIYAZAKI

Ichisada Miyazaki (1901–   ) is one of the foremost Sinologists of Japan today. In his studies he has shown interest not only in a grasp of the whole course of Chinese history but also in an awareness of historical developments in other civilizations of the world. Some of his major works are concerned with institutional developments, such as currency in the Five Dynasties and early Sung periods, the civil service examination system, and the earlier nine-grade ranking system. In monographs and broader interpretive works he has refined the thesis of Naito Torajirō that Chinese society changed from an "aristocratic" one to an "autocratic" one in the course of time from the late T'ang dynasty (618–906) through the Sung; and he has examined the characteristics of the "modern" society that emerged. In the essay given in large part here, he attempts to review the reforms in terms of both the men concerned with them and the historical pressures of the times.

THE TRIBUTE TRANSPORT AND DISTRIBUTION SYSTEM, THE FARMING LOANS, AND THE STATE TRADE SYSTEM

For Wang An-shih, it was to be expected that Sung should excel other countries in such things as size, population, wealth and wisdom. That she should be unexpectedly behind Liao and Hsi Hsia was the fault of government; in fact, it was because the way of the ancient kings was not being carried out. In the ancient period when the way was being carried out, of course, and even during Han and T'ang, China was the center and brought foreign countries under control. From the Five Dynasties on, China held no such sway. This was because China had entered on a mistaken course. It was imperative that there be a return to the true way, that is, to the way taught by the ancient kings. As to what should be the goal, the true teaching reached back as far as Yao and Shun, but since that teaching was not detailed enough, the rites of Chou should be taken as standard. Since, furthermore, there were great differences in periods, it was according to the spirit of the standard that government must be conducted.

Thus the *Rites of Chou* left by the Duke of Chou became his classical authority. In general, if we ask today how much value the Confucian classics had for political reform, since they were produced in a simple society of old, they might seem, for a society troubled by the social and cultural complexities of a later age, hardly more than an Alka Seltzer. From a scholarly viewpoint it would be incorrect to attempt to explain, as often happens in instances of reform in the name of a return to the past, the most complicated ways of thinking of the present in terms of the past. Yet where, as in China, custom was respected highly, in order to overcome certain cus-

From Ichisada Miyazaki, *Ajia-shi kenkyū*, No. 1. Kyoto: Kyoto University. 1957, pp. 254–267. Reprinted by permission of the author. Translated by the editor of this volume.

toms, even older customs had to be cited. Thus it was that the classics were cited, for from Sung on autocratic power increased, and the regulations of the founders bound their descendants with great force. The classics, which had still more authority, had to be cited to combat this.

What actually disturbed Wang An-shih was that finances were not following the right way. It was not simply that there had to be changes because the government's finances were in trouble. Because finances were not following the right way, the resulting trouble extended to all the people; the gulf between rich and poor was enormous, and the children of the Son of Heaven were reduced to great misery. The aim of his new economic policies was not limited to the trivial one of increasing the central government's income.

He was afraid lest in effecting these new policies they might become sucked into the whirlpool of factional dispute. If he described his aspirations in State Council, they would certainly stir up fruitless opposition. Therefore he persuaded Shen-tsung to establish a special office called the Finance Planning Commission, which was directly responsible to the Emperor, and he and others of like mind became directors of it. This was comparable to what we should call today a finance investigation commission. But one complaint in the attack of the opposition against it was that as soon as it found something to be done it established an appropriate organ to do it. Incidentally, the Commission later won Shen-tsung's increasing confidence, to the point that it held as much importance as the Cabinet, which, no longer considered necessary, was abolished.

The Commission's first accomplishment was the Tribute Transport and Distribution System. At the time, materials needed by the capital were transported there from elsewhere, especially south China. The kinds and amounts of materials had in the course of time become fixed. Since the necessities of the central government changed with the times, a discrepancy grew between what

was supplied and what was needed. Goods brought from distant places at much trouble were sold off at sacrifice prices in the capital as not needed. On the other hand, necessary goods were acquired at high prices from merchants, so that for the government both income and disbursement were extremely uneconomical. Despite that, on the part of the people, the goods collected by the government might be needed or not; whichever the case, they must be collected with a great show of diligence. At times, merchants sold goods that had been bought for a trifle in the capital at illegally high prices, giving it out that they were required for taxes. In the troubled ground between the government and the people, exorbitant profits were garnered by merchants.

In order to end this depletion economy contradictory to the principle of government, Wang An-shih enacted the Tribute Transport and Distribution System, said to have been enacted previously by Emperor Wu of Han [r. 140–187]. A close connection was made between the Finance Commission (*san-ssu*), which was the central Ministry of Finance, and fiscal intendants charged with collecting revenues in south China. Annually the Finance Commission was to draw up a budget. On that basis, the fiscal intendants were to collect the needed materials in the needed amounts only, in places which, as much as possible, produced the goods, and as close to the capital as possible. Goods were never to be demanded of the people in places where the goods did not exist. Substitutions could be made of goods most abundantly produced, and if these were not required at the capital, the fiscal intendants could transport them to places that needed them and sell them at profit. When this plan was put into effect, those who suffered most were businessmen who had been excessively profiting from their connections with government up to that time. On the whole, officials were forbidden by law from engaging in commerce, but in fact they exploited their specially favorable position in government and under the name of relatives or other men carried on commercial transactions constantly; or else they accepted bribes from merchants profiting from the government. In officialdom, this kindled the flames of opposition on the grounds that it was competing with the people for profit and was not the kind of thing the Court should do. Among the officials there were some, upright statesmen, who were caught up in this position without realizing the full significance of what they were doing and supported it.

Next was the Farming Loans measure. A money economy was growing gradually at the time. Money rates, moreover, were extremely high. In these circumstances, in spring, before the grain could be harvested and when farmers had nothing on hand to eat or were even having trouble getting seed, they borrowed money from rich men at extremely high interest rates. According to the custom of the time, from spring to fall was counted as one period, in which the interest would be from sixty to seventy per cent. Therefore debt plagued farm villages, and independent cultivators might go under and become tenants. Tenants, tied by debt, might fall almost to the level of agricultural serfs attached to landlords. The Farming Loans measure was one to establish facilities for small money loans to such farmers. The general plan of the measure was to establish two periods in a year, from spring to fall and from fall to spring. People who wanted to borrow money or grain at the beginning of a period could borrow it from the government at the district granary. Security was not especially required, but ten men had to form a group and accept joint responsibility. Often money was lent and grain repaid, which was made possible because every year the government needed huge amounts of grain for military rations and would have had to buy it from the people. If the price of grain was high at repayment time, the government could collect instead a sum of money corresponding to the grain; but, it was said, the government could not take more than twenty per cent above the original principal.

This time the new economic program brought panic among regional landlords. The reason was that landlords were at the same time usurers. They lent money to tenants or poor farmers at rates of from sixty to seventy per cent a period, bringing them under tight and eventually complete control. If their own money-lending activities should be completely disrupted by the government's circulation of money, interest rates would have to drop sharply. Then the fact that they had enjoyed such high rates until then would come to seem immoral. Thus fiery opposition to the Farming Loans measure came from the landlord class. And the majority of officials at Court were landlords at home. Naturally enough, attacks on the Farming Loans system, among all of Wang An-shih's New Laws, were most severe. Of course such elder statesmen as Han Ch'i, Ou-yang Hsiu, and Fu Pi who opposed the measure did not think that their opposition arose from their own class interests. Most likely they were moved by the views of the officials of the whole Court and hastily concluded that this was the opinion of all the people. Poor farmers and tenants, who had no organ to express their opinions, in their sluggishness probably did not even know what discussions were going on at Court.

The submitting by Han Ch'i, elder statesman of three reigns, of a long memorial from Hsiang-chou, requesting the Emperor to give up the idea of enacting the Farming Loans measure, naturally moved Shen-tsung; and apparently there were some among the officials who expected a change of administration. But for Wang An-shih a measure like the Farming Loans was no more than the first step in the administration he envisaged. Even if he made inroads against landlords' profits, that was nothing more than eliminating injustice and restoring things to normal. If this New Law were crippled, how many plans would surely be torn to pieces in the future? Thereupon he staked everything on a gamble. He left the Court on grounds of illness and presently submitted a request to be allowed to resign his post. To the young Emperor, not seeing Wang An-shih even for a short time, there seemed something lacking, even though he carried on discussions with such high ministers as Tseng Kung-liang, Ch'en Sheng-chih, and Chao Pien. He commissioned Wang An-shih's close friend Han Chiang to urge Wang to return to the Court, saying that everything would be in his hands. Ch'eng Hao and other newly risen statesmen furthered this on their own part and encouraged the Emperor that Wang An-shih should not leave.

Wang An-shih, moved by Shen-tsung's heightened confidence, reappeared at the Court and had the Finance Planning Commission examine the contents of Han Ch'i's memorial. He had Han Ch'i's complaints against the Farming Loans measure answered item by item, refuting the arguments, printing the refutation and circulating it. In Wang An-shih's mind, other men's opinions having been worthless, he had disregarded them; but Han Ch'i's memorial was well-reasoned and worthy as an opposition opinion. That being so, Wang took the steps he did in order not to be misunderstood by Han Ch'i. Opposing this, Lü Kung-chu, a colleague of Wang An-shih, said that such behavior was improper, since it had embarrassed Han Ch'i, an elder statesman. If Han Ch'i had been a short-tempered man, he flatly stated, he would have put on his Chin-yang armor [apposite allusion to the actions of a loyal minister in classical times; from the Kung Yang commentary to the *Spring and Autumn Annals* of Confucius] and exterminated the wicked one at the side of the ruler. For this indiscretion, he was dismissed from the capital. Ch'eng Hao, who had become a protégé of his, suddenly changed his attitude after this and opposed the New Laws in recognition of his obligation to Lü Kung-chu.

Discussion having risen to the boiling point, Shen-tsung asked Wang An-shih why. Wang An-shih answered that it was because among the councillors there was opposition, among the censors opposition, and among the regional officials opposition. Once the Emperor asked why it was that so far the most opposed measure had been the Farming Loans. Wang An-shih answered that it was because the Emperor himself had doubts. But many complaints should not be feared; the only question was whether the action was right. In the time of the Duke of Chou, when the act was right, though his brothers disobeyed, the hearts of men were not lost. In the time of Wang Mang [a famous reformer and usurper, r. 9–23], to the contrary, though hundreds of thousands praised his virtue, he did not win the hearts of men. If despite being right one compromises in one step to win adulation from many, one is apt to be swept up suddenly in their common cause. Here we should recognize how firm Wang's conviction was.

Under the Farming Loans measure, merchants and artisans in cities were permitted to borrow money if they wished, but the main object had been farmers. There was then enacted solely for merchants the State Trade System. At times, merchants could not sell their goods immediately, even though they had transported them from outlying districts. In cities there was a wholesale business, with warehouses . . . operated by rich merchants. When someone wanted to convert merchandise quickly into money, he would sell it at wholesale there, but the [operating merchants], mindful of his weak position, would buy at a reduced price. Therefore, since merchants were fearful of loss of this kind they did not move goods, which piled up where they were produced. In the consuming regions, prices rose for lack of goods. Under these conditions rich merchants made huge profits, but since profits were meager for both producers and transporters, production did not increase. In order to stimulate production and transportation, loans had to be made easier for merchants. Therefore trade offices, where merchants could sell goods in surplus or use them as security for borrowing capital, were established in principal cities. The interest on loans was ten per cent a period, twenty per cent a year. If they were not paid up at the end of a period, a monthly fine was added. This comprised the main large-scale circulation of money, but there was also some extremely small-scale lending. That to local food shops is an example: daily they might be lent a certain amount of capital, which had to be repaid before the day was out.

The State Trade System, too, amounted to commercial activities by the government. There was criticism that from of old it had been agreed that the government should not compete with the people for profit. The Emperor also heard that it was being said that lending money even to street-stall vendors was excessively minute and reflected on the dignity of government. To this, Wang An-shih replied that even among officials there were different kinds, some of whom had to handle matters of detail. Officials of prefectures and districts actually were calculating taxes down to pennies. It mattered not at all what detailed work a man who was responsible for details did. On the other hand, it was an error for one who was Emperor to become involved in such detailed matters. He ought only to ask whether or not the matter accorded with reason. Wang's reasoning was of this lucid style, and there was no one at the Court who could match him in debate.

The three systems above were first-aid measures designed to answer to the advances of society of the time and did not touch the foundations of the society. The *Pao-chia* System and Hired-Services System to be discussed next, however, Wang An-shih had put his heart's blood into designing. In their success or failure they would exert no small effect on the whole of Chinese society.

THE PAO-CHIA AND HORSE-BREEDING SYSTEMS

The military system of China had undergone changes from ancient times on, but generally speaking it had been built on the principle of every-man-a-soldier up to

T'ang times. The prefecture (*chou*) had been the unit, and the basic concept had been that the defense of a prefecture was a function of the prefecture. The chief official of a prefecture had been the governor . . . who superintended the army and the people. The regional commanders [of later times] had originally been no more than variations of these governors. From Sung on, the chief official of a prefecture came to be called the prefect. The guardsmen he directed were in fact men who received no military training. The imperial armies, which bore the brunt of war, were under direct control of the central government and were garrisoned outside [in the prefectures] only in times of emergency. Military and civil affairs had become distinctly separated. At the same time the central government had also had to assume full responsibility for the defense of the prefectures. Then, with a degeneration of the central military administration, the imperial armies grew lax and incompetent, and military strength had to be kept up by increasing the numbers of troops as their quality dropped. Because they were professional soldiers, they could not be disbanded at once and sent home to their farms, even though a war might be over. In this way, the numbers of troops gradually grew and strained the Court's finances. From the middle of the Northern Sung period on, this baneful condition was acute, with eighty per cent of the state's funds going to maintain inefficient troops.

To bring order to the entangled state finances, it would be necessary to set to work ordering the military establishment. The question what to do about excessive troops, as even today in the Republic of China, where it is a great problem, seemed so difficult that it was hard to know where to begin. It seemed to Wang An-shih that unless there was something better than using a hired-soldier system, an ultimate settlement would be difficult. His conclusion was that the basis must be the principle of every-man-a-soldier, as in T'ang and before. Since Northern Sung was not far removed from T'ang in time, probably this policy of a return to the past did not seem impossible.

Even in the Sung dynasty, civilian soldiers were not entirely lacking. There were people's organizations . . . in many regions that had suffered from hostile forces, and at times they had been forcibly commandeered by the government and assigned to border defense with imperial armies. In fact, when they had tried out, the results had been rather good. They had a reputation for being more useful than the arrogant imperial armies. Wang An-shih would try to train such civilian soldiers, gradually replacing the imperial armies with them, and return to the old way of a farmer-soldiery.

First he organized people's self-defense groups, calling a group of ten households a *pao,* fifty households a big *pao,* and ten big *pao* a joint *pao,* commissioning a leader over each. In households with two or more able-bodied males, one was designated a *pao*-man and made subject to duty. At first these men were given simple policing duties; if someone in the *pao* committed a crime, they were to arrest him. Soon the *pao*-men were brought together in seasons of little farm work and trained in military skills. Awards were made to those who excelled, and military attitudes were inculcated. Once their military training had been completed they might be assigned, as in the T'ang garrison system, to security stations and used to catch brigands. At first this was begun in the Kaifeng district, near the Emperor, and then was extended to Hopei, Hotung and Shensi circuits, bordering on Liao and Hsi Hsia; and also Kwangsi and Kwangtung, next to Annam.

The training, honoring, and stationing of the *pao* forces required a certain expenditure, which was arranged as follows. When vacancies occurred in the imperial armies owing to old age or death, these openings were not filled, and the funds for them were put aside . . . These "remitted funds" were used for the *pao* forces. In this way, at the same time that order was being brought to the imperial forces, the *pao* forces could be formed in place of them.

Complaints against the *Pao-chia* System arose on all sides, as they had against the other New Laws. But should the scheme be accomplished, the government would be freed of the burden of huge military expenditures. Maintaining only a very small imperial force in peacetime, it could call up tens of millions of good militiamen in event of an emergency. And if military expenditures were lightened, it could revoke such onerous measures as the tea and salt monopolies and give economic relief to the people. Then banditry would naturally decline, and the military establishment, at least for internal security, would become almost unnecessary. However, everything depended on whether the plan could be moved ahead as ordered.

Come to think of it, the connotation of China's modern distinction between soldiers and farmers was different from Japan's. In Japan, soldiers were at the same time samurai; they were aristocrats. When, then, from Meiji times on every man became a soldier, this meant not only an addition to the people's duties but also a rise in their status. In China, however, soldiers were derelicts; the unemployed, menials. Driven from the people, one became a soldier: however many incentives might be devised, should the people's anti-military attitudes not be eradicated, it would be displeasure and hostility. They could be made superficially to acquire the forms of the military arts, but unless they were subjected to a great deal of training it would probably be impossible to turn this mild people into tiger-like braves. On this point the views of Ssu-ma Kuang, the historian, hit the mark, though not by calculation.

Together with the *Pao-chia* System there was the Horse-Breeding System. China having lost pasturage for horses as she brought her land under cultivation, she usually sought war horses from the barbarians of the north. However, when Liao and Hsi Hsia rose they forbade the export of horses, so that it was extremely difficult to procure war horses in the Sung dynasty. At the beginning of the dynasty domestic pasture lands had been established, but the results had been disappointing. Upon effecting the policy of keeping soldiers on the farms under the *Pao-chia,* Wang An-shih also thought of keeping horses among the people; to this end, he initiated the Horse-Breeding System. He encouraged keeping horses among the *pao*-forces' households, and to any who made a request he gave a state horse or money for a horse. In peacetime the horse could be used by the household, but not overworked. For that reason, there was an annual inspection. If a horse had died and the household was rich, a fine of the full price was imposed; half-price if the household was poor. Households that kept the animals were exempted from certain kinds of surtaxes.

This policy, too, seems ultimately to have been unsound. The horses that were necessary to the people were pack horses or draft horses. What was necessary in battle was saddle horses. Even if farm horses were pressed into use in an emergency, they would not serve the purpose. When used by inexperienced Sung forces, we can imagine the results. It would be unthinkable that such men as these should do battle with Liao and Hsi Hsia cavalrymen riding spirited animals that had been grazed on the open plateaus of the north. But after Wang An-shih had retired, the Horse-Breeding System became the Horse-Quartering System: rich people were forcibly ordered to keep horses, and there were not a few incidents of harm and disturbance to the people. Wang An-shih's original idea of the plan, however, had not been to effect it by force.

THE HIRED-SERVICES SYSTEM

The problem of a service system neither began nor ended with Sung, but there was never as noisy a discussion over it as in Sung. The reason surely was that this was a transitional period, after the collapse of the medieval society and before the formation of the modern one.

The "service" of the service system referred to here was not really *corvée.* It was not service for the government undertaken as physical labor by the people for so many days. The physical labor of twenty days done for the state during the T'ang had already been swallowed up in the twice-a-year tax system. This service was different from that.

In the middle ages the influential men of a region not only passed on their wealth from generation to generation but also tended to pass on intact their social position. Thus the richest in a village were the village chiefs from generation to generation; the elders of a quarter represented the quarter from generation to generation. When the ordinary people came up for physical labor, such men led them as their chiefs but did not themselves do physical labor. At tax-collection time, they pressed their people. If there were bandits, they caught them. The village chiefs and representatives stood between the people and the officials, and local self-government was centered on them. Their positions were both duties and privileges.

Later, however, their positions gradually grew only in burdens. First there was the increase in financial aid to the central government, together with the growth of regional wealth. Up to that time, it had been sufficient to send formal tribute to the central government, but now many goods were required. The gathering, supervising and forwarding of such taxes or tax-like things became the responsibility of these locally influential men. If there were mistakes, they themselves had to make compensation. Local officials were, with the strengthening of imperial authority, "district managers" of the central government. Not good officials in relation to the people, they enforced the obligations of localities to the central government harshly, without extenuation. What had until then been a position of honor [that of locally influential men] thereupon became disliked as painful service.

Second was the rise of officials' households. Up to that time, district representatives had been the most exalted persons of districts and village chiefs the most powerful in the villages. But officials' households had risen in districts and villages and did not submit to the control of the chiefs. They were the families of commissioned officials of the Court, who, as they rose in the world through the civil-service examinations or other means, conferred on their families a position almost beyond the law. Exploiting these circumstances, families not only became great landlords but at times did not pay their taxes. Village chiefs were powerless to do anything about this. Feeling pressure from the government, they had no recourse but to sacrifice their own resources instead. Since there was no service as unprofitable as this, everyone tried to avoid it. The result being an obstruction of operations, the government set up positions to take the place of the village leaders. This was the Dispatched-Services System established in the reigns of T'ai-tsu [r. 960–976] and T'ai-tsung [r. 976–997] of Sung.

Under the Dispatched-Services System, various services corresponding to differences in wealth were forcibly required . . . The most burdensome of these was that of "office service"; this was the staffing of public offices. What the men who were sent out to offices did was to guard the storehouses. They were not simply guards, they were responsible for the maintenance of official goods. If the grain rotted or was stolen and the accounts did not tally, they had to make compensation, though it meant giving up their families' property. At times it was ordered that such goods be transported to the capital: on the way the ship might be sunk and a family suddenly ruined. At the beginning of Sung, administration was still firm and officials' families still few, so that the issue was not too great a one, but together with the rapid increase of officials' families the responsibility for

local services was shifted to a small remaining number of reasonably well-off farmers. Gradually the well-off farming families went under one after another, and eventually ones that might be ordered to dispatched services disappeared. For the now casual Sung Court, understandably, this necessarily became a problem.

In Wang An-shih's time discussions over improving the Dispatched Services had already become animated, and at first Ssu-ma Kuang, Su Ch'e and others had championed the need for improvement. Among Wang An-shih's New Laws, only those concerning the service system quite fitted the mood of the times. After carefully conferring repeatedly with Shen-tsung, Wang An-shih revised the Dispatched Services to enact the Hired-Services System. Under it, people were not dispatched to those services that, like "office service," required expending one's own wealth to fulfill. Instead, the government enrolled applicants, paid them a salary and commissioned them in office. Among the people, those whose wealth qualified them for service would pay an exemption charge appropriate to their wealth. Officials' families as well as temples and merchants' families, which until then had been exempted from service, would pay approximately a fifty per cent charge. Men for service were enlisted on the basis of these funds, but it is estimated that income exceeded budgetary requirements by about twenty per cent. The excess was called surplus funds.

The special feature of this new law was its progressive nature. Contrary to the return to the past of the *Pao-chia* System above, this gave up returning to the past and anticipated a different, new society. It freed the people from conditions of feudalistic local government and exacted from them only taxes. It tended to further and extend the division of labor in society. It favored officials' families to some extent, but all in all it acknowledged their position only as one category in the division of labor.

Against this most appropriate Hired-Services System, too, there were criticisms. As storehouse guards, nothing was better than simple farmers; probably salaried guards would line their pockets [with government funds]. Taking the "surplus funds" was a cruelty inflicted on the people. These and others are serious arguments, but at bottom much of what was said was probably a venting of rage at the first imposition of a burden on officials' families, which until then had borne no duties. Su Shih's statement, "If the Hired-Services System is carried out, officials will not be able to let rich farmers entertain them, and there will be no more advantage in being an official," was the unveiled truth. It was just the kind of thing Su Tung-p'o would say.

CRITIQUE OF THE NEW LAWS

All the New Laws produced worthy effects. At the least, finances took a turn for the better. Social order was also improved. There are some writers who ascribe the fall of Northern Sung, the disaster of 1126, to Wang An-shih; but what Chinese dynasty has not fallen? Obviously the fall of Northern Sung was not brought about by Liao, which confronted Sung in Wang An-shih's time and later. If Sung, which had enacted the New Laws, had been destroyed by Liao, which had not enacted New Laws, perhaps that could have been blamed on the New Laws; but Sung was destroyed utterly unexpectedly by Chin, at the same time that Chin destroyed her enemy Liao. The disaster of 1126, moreover, came 170 years after the founding of the dynasty and fifty after Wang An-shih, and, as it is said, its time had come.

If we consider the matter calmly, it was rather the reign of Jen-tsung [1023–1064] that was critical for Sung. That reign, peaceful on the surface, was the period in which general organization was breaking down and even the very life of the nation was in danger, should there be a strong attack. The New Laws were not Wang An-shih's alone, they were the sorrowing cries of the young statesmen whose consciences were not yet paralyzed. But in China reforms have often been eaten away in concessions to the mode of things as they are. Good measures and splendid ideas have been eviscerated. It was extremely regrettable that, under repeated changes in administration from Wang An-shih on, the original ideas were progressively watered down in practice. If there had never been Wang An-shih's reforms, who could have guaranteed that Sung's pulse would surely go on beating those last fifty years?

Reappraisal of Wang An-shih

JAMES T. C. LIU

James T. C. Liu is Associate Professor of History in Stanford University. He has studied modern Sino-Japanese diplomatic relations, but in recent years has given most of his attention to Chinese institutional history, especially the workings of political institutions in the traditional period.

R ECENT scholars have not yet attempted a comprehensive study of Wang and the reform. They have been more inclined to devote themselves to detailed studies of specific reform measures, one by one. They are keenly aware that Wang and the reform can only be understood in the broad frame of reference of his period and the various developmental trends of Sung society. In this regard, important contributions have been made by many scholars, notably the following: Ch'üan Han-sheng on economic history, Miyazaki Ichisada on government and political behavior, Nieh Ch'ung-ch'i on government institutions and political history, Sogabe Shizuo on finance, and Sudō Yoshiyuki on the land system and bureaucratic social mobility.

The attention of the recent scholars in the field of Sung history, collectively speaking, has been given first to the economic development and second to the political institutions. Relatively little has been done on Sung thought. Studies in this last field generally stress the metaphysical and the self-cultivationist philosophies that began to develop in the Northern Sung and became predominant in the Southern Sung.

Conversely, there has been a neglect of the political theories, especially those with a utilitarian emphasis, that were influential during the Northern Sung. Hsiao Kung-ch'üan, while not a Sung specialist, deserves credit for assigning due weight to this aspect in his general history of Chinese political thought.

From all this literature emerge diverse interpretations of Wang and his reform. In the traditional historiography Wang has been regarded as a brilliant scholar, an honest but obstinate statesman, misguided by his excessive self-confidence and his misplaced trust in unworthy associates. In this view, Wang cannot be considered a foremost Confucianist in the orthodox sense. On the other hand, the detailed study by Ts'ai Shang-hsiang contends that this is a misunderstanding, if not a distortion, and that Wang should be regarded as a true and indeed an extraordinary Confucianist.

The publications of the present century, needless to say, no longer base their interpretations of Wang on Confucian grounds. Liang, in his biographical work, emphasizes Wang's ideals and reform measures that aim at "enriching the nation (or the state) and strengthening the army"

Reprinted by permission of the publishers from James T. C. Liu, *Reform in Sung China*, pp. 13–17, 52–58, 114–116. Cambridge, Mass.: Harvard University Press. Copyright, 1959, by The President and Fellows of Harvard College.

91

(*fu-kuo ch'iang-ping*). Other authors, for example, J. C. Ferguson, appraise Wang in the light of modern liberalism. Yet others, notably Williamson, compare Wang's reform to state socialism. In the current era, charged with a nationalistic and revolutionary spirit, the popular interpretations of Wang tend to overglorify him. Only one rare exception, expressing a minority view, regards Wang as "dictatorial," and this work, not being very judicious in its use of historical sources, need not be taken too seriously. In any event, these varied interpretations have one common characteristic: they examine Wang retrospectively through modern glasses and from the particular political viewpoint held by the author.

Research scholars in more recent years have invariably drawn attention to the general developments during the Sung period, with particular emphasis on the socio-economic trends; these socio-economic trends they have used as a basis for interpreting political trends, such as the ones reflected in Wang's reform measures. These scholars stress the vested interests of the scholar-official class in its landownership and privileges. They suggest that in such vested interests lies the clue that explains the bureaucratic character and the absolutist nature of the Sung empire. While they do not deny that Wang was a reformer, praiseworthy, idealistic, and extraordinary, they feel that it would be a mistake and an undue glorification to regard him as an exceptional statesman rising above the socio-economic context of his time.

Two hypotheses are emphasized in the more recent interpretations of Wang and his era that have been offered by such scholars as Naitō Torajirō, Wang Yü-ch'üan, Sudō Yoshiyuki, and several other Japanese researchers who follow Sudō's line of inquiry. The first is that Wang represents the interests of the newly risen medium-sized landowners (located mainly in the southern areas) in a surging and vigorous struggle against the vested interests of large-scale landlords (mainly in the northern areas) and the large and monopolistic merchants. The second is that the New Policies in effect expanded the power of the bureaucratic class as a whole and tightened the control of the absolutist state.

These two hypotheses are not necessarily in disagreement. It has been suggested that a close relationship may be seen to exist between the interests of the medium-sized landowners and the interests of the absolutist state. On the one hand, the medium-sized landowners value the protection of the state; on the other hand, the medium-sized landholding probably accords best with the interests of the absolutist state itself. However, this coincidence of interest by no means implies a complete identity of interest. The recent research of many scholars has effectively demonstrated that the bureaucrats played a double role in serving simultaneously the interests of both the medium-sized landholders and of the absolutist state. No study has yet been made of the choices made by some bureaucrats when these two sets of interests conflicted. Wang through his New Policies probably tried to serve the best interests of the state as he idealized them, sometimes even at the expense of the class to which he belonged by social origin. Yet many of his followers probably identified themselves less with the state's interests than with their class, if not their personal, interests.

The recent interpretations so far have clarified considerably, though not yet conclusively, the general socio-economic trends of the time. It is still questionable whether the class-interest hypotheses in these interpretations are fully supported by factual findings; alternatively it is possible that the socio-economic trends posited by such hypotheses, if substantiated, will offer sufficient explanations of the political trends. While socio-economic factors unquestionably influence political trends, there are other factors which also play their part and these have to be assessed. The recent interpretations have not given enough attention, for instance, to the diverse lines of thought or political philosophies which divided the scholar-officials into different and opposing schools. Furthermore, political trends have dynamics of their own. To the same socio-economic setting and even within one given school of thought, scholar-officials respond with different political behavior. Such behavior provides a basis for classifying them into distinctive bureaucratic types. In short, the recent interpretations, though enlightening and helpful, still leave considerable room for a reappraisal. . . .

Wang had the rare opportunity, enjoyed by few statesmen in history, of putting many of his ideas into actual practice. For he enjoyed the almost unreserved trust of the Emperor from the beginning of the reform in 1069 to the time of his temporary resignation from the court in 1074. The only political opposition that disturbed him was the incessant criticism of the censors, and these, on the insistence of Wang, were demoted one after another.

The improvement of custom by government initiative. The task Wang defined for himself was fourfold: "the production of well-trained personnel, the further improvement of state finance, the change to better customs, and the issuance of better orders and laws." The most fundamental of these was the improvement of custom through the regulatory systems to be instituted by the government. Wang repeatedly used the expression "custom" (*feng-su*) as a keynote in discussing policies with the Emperor, and the Emperor, evidently under his influence, did the same. However, there is evident in his writings a crucial change in the meaning of the word "custom." In the writings before he assumed power, the term referred to social custom in general. In his discussions at the court, it referred principally to the practices and political behavior among the bureaucrats, or in other words, the "political custom" of the bureaucracy in particular. Among his numerous comments to the Emperor, the following

two are especially revealing. On one occasion Wang commented on the prevailing practices and attitudes of the bureaucrats:

The worst defect in the present practices is the lack of loyalty (*chung*) and honesty (*hsin*) and the disregard of financial integrity (*lien*) and sense of honor (*ch'ih*). A man like Ch'ang Chih conducts himself admirably and should be praised and honored. To keep him at the court helps to set a good example and promote good practices.

This comment was in perfect accord with the belief of the conservatives. But Wang did not mean to stop there. On another occasion he discussed the relative importance of improving practices among the bureaucrats and "enriching the state and strengthening the army." He came to the conclusion that they were equally important:

What Wu Ch'i [of the Warring Kingdom Period] did in enriching the state and strengthening the army is naturally not the way of virtuous men (*chün-tzu*). . . . The ancient kings, having improved upon their government policies and made their state sufficiently strong, took steps to perfect the customs so that their descendants, even when faced with the hardship of poverty or the crisis of disruption in the succession to the throne, would have no rebellious disturbance. To make no effort to promote loyalty, honesty, financial integrity and sense of honor, but to concentrate on strengthening the state—that was the failure of the Ch'in empire. On the other hand, to make no effort to improve upon the government policies, but to concentrate on rewarding those who were chaste, righteous, financially clean and admirably modest—that was the failure of the late Han empire. In both cases, the mistake was to lean toward the one, neglecting the other.

Wang's opinion is quite clear. The utilitarian policies are the immediate tasks; but moral improvement remains, as all Confucianists believe, the ultimate goal. Both are necessary conditions of good government; neither is sufficient in itself. As a matter of fact, Wang kept on reminding the Emperor that, in spite of all the New Policies already introduced, one fundamental reform was yet to be carried out, namely a change toward higher standards of conduct.

Regulatory systems and laws. Wang differed from his conservative opponents in yet another important respect. It was his conviction that the desired change toward higher standards of conduct could not be achieved by moral education alone. It would require an improvement in popular custom which must be regulated by more effective institutional controls. The government should participate actively in setting up various regulatory systems and in promulgating good laws. This was exactly what the ancient sagacious emperors had done, and it should not be confused at all with the emphasis upon mere laws or mainly upon rewards and punishments that was peculiar to the Legalists. In fact, judging from the government activities under Wang it is more correct to say that the reform stressed the need for better administrative systems more than the need for effective laws. During the reform phase, the government accounting system was revised and 400 fascicles of the rules and regulations of the Finance Commission were compiled. Officials were appointed to study administrative procedures and problems. The government also ordered a new codification of the laws and the decrees, but this was not regarded as particularly important.

With regard to the application of the laws, Wang himself considered the codes too severe and the use of capital punishment excessive. It cannot be denied that in the promotion of the reform measures many violators were frequently penalized by law. But this is attributable more to the officials foregoing the usual means of nonlegal suasion, rather than to the New Policies or their intention. It should also be noted that after Wang's first resignation Lü Hui-ch'ing, who succeeded him, hardly discussed the long-range objective of promoting better practices and good social customs. Lü did not even introduce further changes in the administrative system but directed his attention mainly to administrative measures and laws.

The classification of Wang as a Legalist was a matter of opinion. Some of his opponents compared him to Wang Mang, the usurper and reformer of the Han period who deviated from Confucianism through his incorrect interpretation of the *Chou-li.* Other opponents regarded Wang An-shih as no less than a Legalist who followed the teachings of Han-fei-tzu and the policies of Shang Yang of the Ch'in kingdom in "enriching the state and strengthening the army." However, these were minority opinions at the time. The strongest attacks upon Wang and the reform were directed toward the state financing policies as profit-seeking operations, undertaken by profit-minded and unscrupulous officials in defiance of general opinion, and causing great disturbance and suffering among the common people. Many opponents, like Ssu-ma Kuang, still recognized Wang as a Confucianist, though a misguided one, rather than as a Legalist.

It was the Southern Sung scholars who later reached the conclusion that Wang was either a Legalist in disguise or came rather close to being one. Even then, the philosopher Chu Hsi, who was not altogether favorable to the New Policies, dissented. By this time the crux of the problem lay in a definition of terms. Some of Wang's critics alleged that the word *fa* and the expression *fa-tu,* which Wang used frequently, essentially meant law, or law and measures, and therefore Wang should be classified as a Legalist. Yet, when numerous passages either in Wang's writings or in his oral comments are examined closely in their context, it is hard thus to restrict the meaning of the word *fa* and the expression *fa-tu* to this specific sense. The more inclusive rendering of "regulatory systems" is probably closer to Wang's real meaning.

Enriching the state and strengthening the army. Confucius himself advocated sufficient food for the people and sufficient defense of the state. Toward the end of the nineteenth century, a number of Confucianists also emphasized these needs. However, according to most, if not all, Confucianists, the Legalists were those who overemphasized the desirability of "enriching the state and strengthening the army" and who sought to attain this objective by expediency instead of through moralistic policies. The question here is whether or not Wang in actual administration did move in the Legalist direction. Wang was in favor of enriching the state through various financial measures. According to his concept of expanding finance, government spending to promote general economic growth would in turn bring into the treasury revenues in excess of expenditures; "there need be no worry of fund shortage" at all. Under the New Policies the state acquired surplus funds and used them to finance additional activities. The cardinal objective of Wang's financial policy was neither the welfare of the farmers nor the elimination of monopolistic trade interests, but the financial security of the state itself. Wang assumed that the state was the organized body ideally representing the totality of the country. Its interests therefore would come before the interests of the common people as individuals.

However important it was to enrich the state, this task, to Wang, was only one among many. The reform of the bureaucracy in order to insure a better administration of all measures, and the improvement of custom through moral influence were of more basic importance and should never be neglected. Unfortunately, the circumstances were such that Wang was unable to make much progress toward these long-range goals. Among other reasons, the Emperor exerted considerable pressure on Wang to give primary attention to the urgent problem of state finance, first to wipe out the deficit and then to meet the increasing demand for funds. Wang probably did overemphasize the objective of enriching the state, but not entirely of his own choice.

On strengthening the army, the Emperor and Wang clearly differed. It was always the Emperor who brought military affairs and strategy up for discussion. He was quite sensitive about the military weakness of his empire and rather anxious to have this situation remedied. Wang agreed to the desirability of territorial expansion at the expense of minority groups in the west, in the south, and in the southwest. But he was opposed to attacking either the Hsi Hsia kingdom on the northwest or the Liao empire on the north. On many occasions when the Emperor initiated a discussion of the army, Wang countered with the advice that financial strength must come before military strength and internal reform before external expansion.

The *pao-chia* policing system, though highly significant, was not as important to the government policy at the time as is sometimes believed; nor was it exactly the forerunner of a conscription system, as some interpretations maintain. It was originally introduced for the prime purpose of maintaining local order and of protecting property rights. When organized, the *pao-chia* policing system also facilitated census taking and tax collection, and helped to eliminate tax evasion. The use of *pao-chia* units as reserve forces in time of war came later, and this never did become their dominant function. In short, Wang was far more in favor of enriching the state than of strengthening the army. And neither was nearly as important to Wang as the reform of the bureaucracy, and the effort of the bureaucracy to set up regulatory systems that would ultimately promote better social customs. In action Wang remained largely true to his theories, which we have described as expressive of a sort of idealism—hoping to use a well-organized bureaucracy for the realization of a moral society. . . .

This reappraisal has shown Wang An-shih as a bureaucratic idealist who upheld the ideal of a professionally well-trained and administratively well-controlled bureaucracy as the principal instrument for the realization of a Confucian moral society. It has also described him as an institutional reformer, who endeavored not only to change government institutions but also to found new ones in order to guide and shape the behavior of both bureaucrats and the people. Wang's principal emphasis was not upon the promulgation and enforcement of law. Nor did he believe the objective of "enriching the state and strengthening the army" to be of prime importance. His ultimate goal was to improve the social customs of the people, looking toward a perfect social order. For these reasons, he and those who agreed with him at the time, as well as those who admired him in later centuries, denied that he was a Legalist. However, the majority of conventional Confucianists believed that the emphasis should be placed upon individual officials rather than upon the bureaucracy. To them, what Wang meant by regulatory systems—or in our words, government institutions and government-initiated institutions—were of the same nature as law. Consequently, they considered Wang a Legalist or at least a misguided Confucianist who had strayed in the same direction as the Legalists. In all fairness, in terms of the theoretical justifications upon which Wang based his views and in terms of his ultimate goal of a moral society, we may still regard Wang as essentially a Confucianist. He was of course a radical Confucianist, but radical only in comparison with many conservative Confucianists.

Since his idealism was basically bureaucratic, Wang always put the interests of the state, as he interpreted them, above everything else. He did not develop a clear definition of his objectives in terms of their effects upon the various social classes. He thought he was helping the majority of the population; yet the improvement of the state finances which the New Policies

brought about was probably far greater than the benefits they brought to the people. While the bureaucratic families and large landowners complained about some features of the New Policies that were objectionable to them, many medium-sized landowners and other less well-to-do people had their share of complaints on other grounds. In short, Wang's policy was neither clearly nor firmly built upon a well-defined social basis.

In Wang's view the bureaucracy was especially important. Yet, precisely on this point he failed, for he did not obtain strong enough support from the bureaucrats. He did not even succeed in inspiring a sustaining loyalty among the executive type of bureaucrats, upon whom he depended principally to carry out the New Policies. What the New Policies did achieve was lost when some of these bureaucrats degenerated into the manipulative type. Furthermore, Wang was theoretical in policy matters rather than practical in politics. He gave far more attention to administration than to the winning over of his opponents, as for example, of the southwestern moderates, who opposed him less vehemently than did the northern conservatives. Thus, though he emphasized the importance of the bureaucracy, he did not really carry the support of the bureaucracy at all.

The bureaucracy performed its service through the government's operations and here Wang's program ran into additional difficulties: growing absolutism, increasing centralization with its attendant danger of power manipulation, greater conformity which was neither politically nor administratively desirable, and the gradually expanding but ever incorrigible clerical subbureaucracy which did not carry out the policies as intended. From the reform, through the antireform, to the postreform, these difficulties became steadily greater, to a degree never anticipated by Wang.

China was a bureaucratic state. Wang was indeed outstanding, if not exceptional, in his emphasis upon utilitarian statecraft, upon the bureaucracy, and upon the gov-

ernment institutions and government initiated institutions. Since his approach did
not succeed, the only alternative seemed to
be that of conventional Confucianism or
what, from the Southern Sung period on,
was respected as orthodox Confucianism.
Yet this latter approach stressed the moral
qualities and the moral influence of the
bureaucratic class and disregarded utilitarian policies and manipulative attitudes
toward the state machinery.

One cannot help asking whether such a
moralistic approach was sufficiently real-
istic. Did it not gloss over the facts of life
in a bureaucratic state and thereby inhibit
later Chinese thinking about political institutions?

SUGGESTIONS FOR ADDITIONAL READING

Useful general bibliographies of the history of the Sung dynasty may be found in Charles O. Hucker, *China: A Critical Bibliography* (University of Arizona Press, 1962), and L. C. Goodrich and H. C. Fenn, *A Syllabus of the History of Chinese Civilization and Culture* (New York: The China Society of America, sixth edition, revised, 1958). For advanced students, the bibliography in James T. C. Liu, *Reform in Sung China* (Cambridge: Harvard University Press, 1959), lists sources in Chinese and Japanese not included in suggestions below. Similarly, a great source of facts, most of them correct, must be mentioned: the article on the Sung dynasty in *Tōyō rekishi daijiten* (Tokyo: Heibonsha, 1941), Vol. V, pp. 287–323).

There are limited resources in European languages. For an introduction to institutional features of the Sung dynasty, Edwin O. Reischauer and John K. Fairbank, *East Asia: The Great Tradition* (Boston: Houghton Mifflin Company, 1960), is the most recent and best interpretive work. L. Carrington Goodrich, *A Short History of the Chinese People* (New York: Harper & Brothers, third edition, 1959), is especially good for cultural innovations. Kenneth Scott Latourette, *The Chinese: Their History and Culture* (New York: The Macmillan Company, 1949), has much sound factual detail.

Among studies directly concerned with the reform and conditions relevant to it, intellectual considerations are examined in Wm. Theodore de Bary, "A Reappraisal of Neo-Confucianism," in *Studies in Chi-nese Thought,* ed. Arthur F. Wright (Chicago: University of Chicago Press, 1953). There are useful introductions to the readings on the Confucian revival in Wm. Theodore de Bary, Wing-tsit Chan, and Burton Watson, *Sources of Chinese Tradition* (New York: Columbia University Press, 1960), pp. 411 ff. Institutional features are studied in E. A. Kracke, Jr., *Civil Service in Sung China, 890–1067* (Cambridge: Harvard University Press, 1953), and the same scholar's "Sung Society: Change within Tradition," in *Far Eastern Quarterly,* 14:479–488 (1955). Johanna M. Menzel's *The Chinese Civil Service: Career Open to Talent?*, a volume in this series, examines aspects of that institution in Chinese society and civilization. James T. C. Liu has examined reform in "An Early Sung Reformer: Fan Chung-yen," in *Chinese Thought and Institutions,* ed. John K. Fairbank (Chicago: University of Chicago Press, 1957). He has also suggested a typology of bureaucrats in "Eleventh-Century Chinese Bureaucrats: Some Historical Classifications and Behavioral Types," in *Administrative Science Quarterly* 4 (September, 1959), 207–226; and "Some Classifications of Bureaucrats in Chinese Historiography," in *Confucianism in Action,* eds. D. S. Nivison and A. F. Wright (Stanford: Stanford University Press, 1959). He offers a cyclical interpretation of Northern Sung rule in "An Administrative Cycle in Chinese History," in *The Journal of Asian Studies* 21:2 (February, 1962), pp. 137–152.

IA 3017

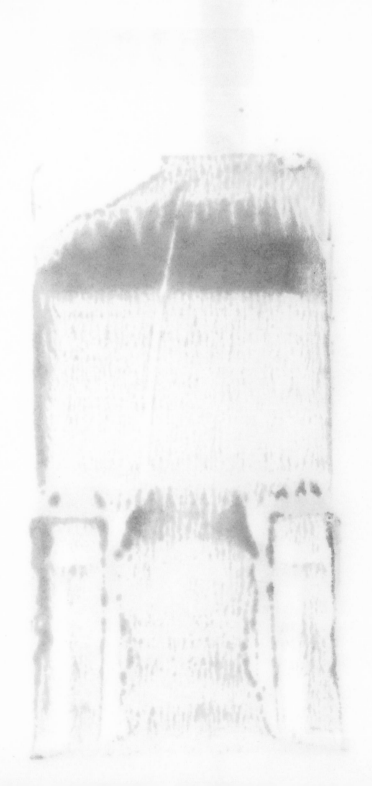